LIFE AFTER MY STROKE

LIFE AFTER MY STROKE

By
Joanna Barnes

authorHOUSE®

AuthorHouse™
1663 Liberty Drive
Bloomington, IN 47403
www.authorhouse.com
Phone: 1-800-839-8640

First published by AuthorHouse   05/20/2011

ISBN: 978-1-4567-8168-2 (sc)
ISBN: 978-1-4567-8169-9 (ebk)

Printed in the United States of America

This book I dedicate to my husband, David because he has put up with a lot over the years we have been married.

I also thank the writer of the gentleman who wrote the next poem and the poem at the end of the book, John Dennett. Who is a blind English teacher in America, who has helped me a lot with this book. Here is the poem:

The Stroke of Time, Luck or Jo

I stumbled and being my treacherous tumble fearing of my foreseeable crumble.
My anxious call was lost as I took that spiralling fall as I passed through that translucent wall.
As it all passed me by, I begin to cry because now, where were my mother, my father and my forever caring brother?
I flew above the clouds and into the sun, never knowing such joyous fun.
I was rushing here and rushing there but, really going nowhere
When out of thin air you were there, letting me know how much you really did care.
You offered your strength; you offered your love which is all from above.
Even though I could not talk or even walk, you helped me talk,
You helped me walk by taking my pains, and the evermore binding chains.
Once, my earthly father was there, even though he did despair,
You gave him the strength to bare and fore me care.
You gave me renewed life by allowing me to be this good man's
Wife the day you placed him my way for you sent him to me with unconditional love, that only comes from above.
So, when my heart touches his pure heart,
I knew that we would never be apart,
I daily remind us to always remember that whenever it thunders or we may make blunders
Rain or shine,
You will always be mine,
Even though someday, we may be far apart,
We will always be one heart,
Although we may have a bad day,

Our hearts will never go astray,
Because you're like an angel from above,
Which was sent to me with love be it by the stroke of time, the stroke
of luck or the stroke of Jo
Who's to know???

I was brought up in a town called Addlestone, which is in the county of Surrey in England. I used to live in a block of maisonettes. There were three sets of maisonettes, Middlesex Court, Sussex Court and Hampshire Court (the one I used to live in). Just across the road was the only block of flats in Addlestone, this was called Surrey Towers; there was sixteen floor in this block of flats. Just down the road from us was the local Police Station, where I did my work experience. I really wanted to join the police force, when I was old enough. It was my biggest ambition to join the police force because of the work that they did, but some dreams never come true. I did my work experience six weeks at the local police station before my life changed over night.

Let me tell you about my family. I lived at number 15 Hampshire Court, with my mum (Jacqueline or Jackie for short), my dad (Keith), my two brothers, Stephen (the eldest) and Kevin (the youngest) and I can not forget the two cats Jonsey and Pepper. Jonsey was a large pure black cat, and Pepper was a small tabby cat. Jonsey liked to sleep on my bed at night, but when he did this he used to take half my bed up, whereas Pepper slept on my mum and dad's bed and she slept between my parents to stop them from doing anything naughty, as if they would! My mum was a large woman in weight but only 5foot 3inches tall, she had brownish hair but was going grey fast but was always dyeing it different colours. One time she went to dye it a dark reddish colour but it came out a bright red instead. The work my mum did twenty years was the local crossing person (a lolly-pop lady), and she used to be a dinner lady, but she packed this job in because she said it was too much for her. She was one of those women who think they know it all when in fact they do not. My dad is a very thin man, about 5foot 5inches tall with brown hair with a hint of ginger in it, he was also very fit. The work that my dad did was he was a milkman. He had been doing this job for many years, since 1973/74-2010. I often use to take the mickey out of my mum and dad because of their size. For instance, if you put my mum and dad together you would say my dad looked like a rake. My two brothers were both taller than me; mind you anyone is taller than me, me being 4ft 11 and two thirds or it would be easier to say I was just under 5 foot. They both had brown hair; my elder brother had a bit of a belly, well he did the last time I saw him he did and my younger brother had a bit of mussel, as I said he did the last time I saw him he did. They took after my mum in that way, where as I took after both my parents. My mum: I have a line across my nose and my dad: it only notices if I don't wear lipstick because my top lip is slightly two different colours.

Then there were my two grandmothers, Dorothy Hoy (my mum's mum) and Joan Norgate (my dad's mum). Dorothy was a little tubby woman (no way near as big as my mum) with grey/white hair and about 5 foot tall, about my height. Joan was a thin woman with ginger hair with a hint of grey, who was about 5 foot 6 inches tall. Both of my grandfathers died when I was about seven or eight. My Granddad Hoy was a tubby man with hardly any teeth. I still think of him because he was my favourite granddad. My Granddad Norgate was a tall man, I can not remember much about him. There was also my Uncle Ted (my mum's younger brother) he was a bit on the tubby side but I would not say he was fat but then I would not say he was slim and he had brown hair with bit of grey in it. Oh, I nearly forgot my Nan Hoy's dog called Brandy. He was a mongrel but a lovely dog. He was a sort of brown/black with more white in him. When every Brandy came over to my mum's house and Pepper was about Brandy used to be afraid of Pepper, because Pepper used to frighten Brandy even though Pepper used to be at least 5 times smaller than Brandy.

I had many friends at school, but one true friend who I still keep in contact with now, her name is Sandy. Sandy had blonde hair but was always slightly bigger build than me. When we were small people mistook us for twins because we looked alike. We have known each other since we were born; we used to live almost next door to each other. I can remember *the* one and only fight we had. It was when we were about eight years old, we fought over something silly but the fight was really serious, I can remember I pulled some of Sandra's hair out. But even after that I am not sure who won, I don't think anyone did, but we have stayed best friends.

The other friends I made with other pupils and teachers are as follows: Lynda, Frances, Mel (now my sister-in-law), Melanie, Caroline, Leigh, Elke, Darren, Mr Chambers (my form tutor and my Duke of Edinburgh Award organizer), Mr Brown & Mr Trigwell (CDT & Technical drawing teachers), Mr Hickford (RE & Political studies teacher), Miss Stocker (now married), Mrs Heron (Music), Mr Allum (Maths, Chess & Archery Instructor for Duke of Edinburgh Award) and Mr Gooch (Art teacher).

I mentioned that Mr Chambers was my Duke of Edinburgh organizer, because a few weeks before that night that everything changed I went to collect my bronze certificate, which I was proud of. In case you have never heard of the Duke of Edinburgh Award scheme I will tell you about what you have to do to gain your bronze award.

It is a scheme for anyone between the ages of 14-25. For this you have to do four things to gain your award. There are three levels of awards to gain, bronze, silver and gold. For the bronze you have to do:-

1) ***Expedition.*** For this you have to do a 30 mile hike over two days, sleep out in a tent (which you put up yourself) and make a meal over a stove. Do some map reading and follow a plan using a compass.

2) ***Skill***. For this you can do anything you like. I did Chess because I have been playing since I was about 7 or 8 and I wanted to improve myself.

3) **_Physical Recreation._** For this you can do anything physical. I did archery because I had never done this before and I want a challenge.

4) **_Service._** For this you can do anything as long as it is a service to somebody or something. As I mentioned before I liked the police, so I did this for my service.

It took me a little longer to finish my bronze award because I broke my right arm when I was fourteen. When I was sixteen, just before my stroke, I collected my bronze award from a school in Stains.

Before I went up to collect my bronze award I went on my work experience at the local police force, I really enjoyed it. The first day I spent on the police patrol cars; they took me all the way up to the headquarters in Guildford, and showed me around the station in Addlestone, Surrey. It was brilliant; I have never been in a place like this before. The second day I spent just down the road from where I live, in the police station, in the radio room. It got a bit boring after a while, but I stuck it out. The third day I spent it at the Magistrate Courts in Cherstsey, Surrey. There I sat in the main court listening to the different cases, it was very interesting. And on the fourth day I was out on the beat with one of the policemen, and we walked all the way up to New Haw, around there and stopped a midwife and asked her if she minded if we checked her car for any faults, she replied no it gave her chance to catch up on some book work. So the policeman showed me what he checked for and how he did it, I watched.

Anyway back to my life story. It all beginnings . . . .

_1988_

It was on a Friday night in March. I went to my youth club like usual. This particular night we all played volley ball. The youth club was run by a school friend's parents. It was a volley ball night. I do not remember, my friends told me. The youth club was situated in the church hall out the back of the church, we played volley ball in the church itself, as the hall out the back was not tall enough.

I do not remember any of this night as most of my life before my stroke is what people have told me. I suppose this is a good thing really because I have nothing to relate to remind me of what I used to be like.

I went home about 9.30pm that was when my dad picked me up in our reliant. Later that night or should I say early next morning, I got up to go to the toilet. My mum asked who that was. Because she always asked if she was awake, I did not answer. Then she heard a thud on the floor, so she quickly got out of bed and went to the bathroom. She found me on the floor being sick and unconscious. She called to me dad to call for an ambulance. At the same time he woke my brother Stephen. The ambulance came they took me to my local hospital in Chertsey, Surrey. I do not know what happened at the hospital, I do know that I was taken from St Peter's Hospital, Chertsey to the Adkinson Morley Hospital in Wimbledon. My brother, Stephen followed behind in his car with my dad sitting next to him; my mum was in the ambulance next to me.

While I was in the Adkinson Morley I spent the first two weeks in a coma in the Intensive Care department. While I was in this part of the hospital I gave everyone a scare or two because my heart stopped three times, but as you can see I am still here alive and kicking. The only people who were allowed to visit me in the Intensive Care department were my mum, my dad and my Nan Hoy (my mum's mum). My other Nan Norgate was not allowed to go in as there is some stupid rule that says that only the mother's mum is only allowed to visit people in Intensive Care but my Nan Hoy let my other Nan go in instead of her, once or twice.

The first thing I remember was when I was in a bed (I had no idea where I was), I went to get out of bed to go to the toilet. As I went to stand I just fell to the floor. I could not stand or walk. What was wrong with me? Why could I not do this? HELP! I had lost my sense of balance. I could not even speak. I couldn't even ask anyone for help. I couldn't even cry. Why couldn't I even do that, a simple thing like that; I did not even know my name. What was wrong with me? Why couldn't I even answer these simple questions? HELP!! Where am I? What sort of place am I in? HELP!!! I want someone to tell me where I am? What I am? I don't know what I am, who I am? Help!!!

The next thing I remember was this strange woman coming over to me (she was not dressed like the other ladies who looked after me) and sitting down; she started to talk to me. I did not know what she was talking about, but whatever she was saying was going in one ear and going out the other. I had no idea who she was, (it was my mum) but she fed me when meal time came. I was thankful for that as I had no idea what a knife and folk was or how to use them either. I had no idea who any of my family was; come to think of it I didn't know I had a family, who were all these people. For a start I had no idea this person who was helping to feed me was my mum, for all I knew she could be the cats mother let alone my mum.

With the time I spent in the hospital I learnt to stand a little but only for a short time. I had also learnt to walk a short distance with the help of two physiotherapists, but without their help I could not walk a step. I had also learnt I had some family, there was my mum (Jackie), my dad (Keith), my two brothers (Stephen and Kevin), my Nan Hoy and my Uncle Ted. With my brothers I only got to see my younger brother Kevin because Stephen was always at work when my so called family came to visit me. But that didn't bother me as I didn't know him anyway.

I spent two weeks in the hospital and the only word I had learnt to say was 'Yes'.

Then they moved me to the Wolfson Centre next door to the hospital. This was a centre for some of the patients from the hospital to go to before they went home. When I went to this centre I was pushed over there in a wheelchair, as at this time I could not walk. When I got there they put me into a life and we went down one floor and along a corridor then into this room with two beds and two wash basins in it. It also had a built-in wardrobe with two doors with two locks in them. There were two wooden chairs; I had the choice of beds so I pointed to the one next to the window.

After I had settled into my room I went upstairs in my wheelchair in the lift and round the corner to the rest room in my wheelchair, where everyone went after they had done all their different activities for each day before they went for their tea.

One person I met when I first went into the Wolfson Centre was Nurse Joe, he was like a giant compared to me. He must have been at least 6 foot 6 inches, with long hazel brown hair tied back. I liked this nurse because he was friendly and kind; that was what I liked about a place like this, there was not a horrible nurse or doctor anywhere in sight.

I met some of the patients while I was there, one was this man his name was Mike Gunn. He was a slim man with short brown hair. He was in there because he was involved in an accident with a police car. The police officer opened the car door while Mike was going past on a bicycle. He was such a funny fellow to be around, always laughing and joking about himself. Another was Albert. He was in his 50's. He was a kind man because he used to push me around the centre, until he left the centre to go home. Another was Dick. He was a tall, tubby man with a beard.

Before Albert left to go home all the other inmates that were going to leave at the same time asked if they could hold a bar-be-q to show their thanks for all their hard work, so they did on a Friday evening after all the classes had finished. My parents and Kevin were allowed to stay for the bar-be-q as well. Kevin enjoyed himself at the bar-be-q because he could help himself to as much as he could eat, so could my mum, I only had two hot dogs as I was not a very big eater.

To the left is Albert with me sitting on his knee, he is dressed in cowboy type clothing because he used to go to country and western weekend events when he used to go home at weekends. The gentleman next to him used to drive him home because he had problems driving.

After Albert left Dick started to push me around the centre grounds. This I didn't mind at first because it was alright, but then he began to push me around outside. When Dick pushed me around he used to take me to a certain place on the grounds and assault me. He used to put his hand down my top and play with my left breast. This happened five days a week for three weeks. I never told anyone about this as all I could say was 'Yes', even if I wanted to say 'No'. The only way I could let anyone know if I want to say 'No' is to shake my head. That is one thing that will haunt me until I die. The only way I could get away from him is to walk, so I was more determined than ever to walk.

I spent about five months in this centre. I used to go home at weekends, Friday to Sunday evenings. One Friday evening I had a school certificate evening to go to. This was to give everyone their certificates for their exams. I did not take any of my exams because I was ill in hospital, so I don't know why I was there. They passed me on six out of nine of my exams because they based it on my course work and my mock exams. The reason why they did that was because I was in the first year (1988) to take the GCSE examinations. The grades I got are as followed:

English (D)
English Literature (D)
Science (C)
Home Economics (Child Development) (F)
Art and Design (E)
CDT: Design and Communication (D)

As you can see that I got my best grade for Science, but that was one of my worst subjects. My best subject was CDT: Design and Communication because that was technical drawing which I really enjoyed. The only subject I would have liked to have got an exam grade for was Mathematics, but I was one piece of course work short. The other two subjects that I did not get a grade for were French and Social & Political Studies. I didn't mind as I was not much good at these two.

Anyway back to that evening out. All the pupils' names were put into groups. It was time for me to get into position, my friend Mel helped me as I found it difficult to walk. Mel is a nice person, she was a tubby girl who was taller than me, and mind you everybody is taller than me. It was my turn to go onto the stage to get my certificates but first I had to go up a small flight of stairs. As I began to climb up the stairs with Mel's help everyone started to clap at me as we went on. I could not understand why they clapped but as I got my certificates instead of shaking my hand the important gentleman just gave me my certificates and joined in with everyone else and clapped. So I then turned to go off the stage with Mel's help. After all the certificates were given out there was some refreshments, I did not want to stay as I was feeling so tired as this was the latest I had been up for along time. Before we left a few of my teachers came up to me and said how glad they were to see me, shortly after we left.

While I was in the Wolfson Centre the activities I did were Physiotherapy and Speech Therapy. I did the Physiotherapy three times a day for five days a week and the Speech Therapy once a day for five days a week. The Physiotherapy was hard work but I enjoyed doing some of the activities they got me to do, like standing up and kicking a ball with my right foot. I enjoyed doing this especially when the ball went all the way down the corridor and the physiotherapist had to go and get it. Another thing I used to like doing in the Physiotherapy was walking up and down the stairs they had in one of the gyms. I did not like doing the speech therapy because it was hard work trying to speak because it gave me a headache. One time it hurt my head so much that it gave me a bad migraine that lasted for three or four days. It was so bad that they had to transfer me back to the main hospital for two days.

While I was in the Wolfson Centre I had me right leg in plaster. Don't worry I did not brake it. It was to straighten my right ankle and foot, because they were bent because off the stroke. Mind you it was not on there that long, one day. I just could not bear it on there much longer than one day. It hurt me so much the pain from my ankle I had to have it taken off. So Nurse Joe came and took it off for me in the middle of the night.

At weekends I used to leave the Wolfson Centre to spend time at home with my family (well I think that they are my family, at least they called themselves my family). During one week my favourite Uncle Harry and Aunt June (I think that they are my favourite Uncle and Aunt, that's what my mum said anyway) came up to visit me, it was a nice surprise. On the way up they saw notices for the circus to be shown at Woking and they wondered if I would like to go, so they asked my mum who said yes I would, without even asking me; but I didn't mind as I don't remember ever seeing the circus. So my Uncle Harry paid for my mum, my dad, my younger brother Kevin and me to go to the circus.

It was not like what I remember seeing a circus to be like in cartoons and on films with clowns, tigers, lions, elephants, horses, etc. But this circus had clowns and an elephant and a couple of horses, apart from that it were just people doing different acts. It is all due to the new regulations of keeping animals. After the circus had finished they were doing a photo with the elephant, so my mum got a photo with Kevin, me and the elephant. Apart from not seeing the tigers and other animals I thought it was quite a good circus.

It was like another weekend I can remember, my Uncle Harry and Aunt June came to my home to pick me up to take me to their house in Henfield, West Sussex. We had a great weekend, as they lived near Brighton we spent one day down there, me in my wheelchair and Uncle Harry, Aunt June and the two girls, Sophie and Annabell walking beside me. We went in to see the dolphins; that was great because the girls hadn't seen them until now and I had never seen them before, so it was a surprise for all three of us. It was a shame that weekend had to end but all good things come to an end.

One day back at the centre, I left my wheelchair by my bed and walked up six flights of stairs to breakfast, it took me some time but I managed to do it. I walked around to the physiotherapy rooms. Later, I walked around to the speech therapy room for my speech lesson, it was so hard, some days especially for someone who is trying to learn how to speak and finding it so hard. But I was getting the hang of walking, but at the end of the day I was tired but I was getting there. From that day onwards at the centre I walked, the only time the wheelchair came out was when I was at home at weekends.

After being in the centre for what seemed like forever but it was only five months, I was allowed to go home. My dad came to pick me up. On the way home we stopped at the local wheelchair centre, in Chertsey, Surrey, to get me a wheelchair for my permanent use, even though I was walking around the centre my mum wanted to get me a wheelchair, I don't know why I wanted to walk everywhere but my mum knows best.

My walking was coming along with leaps and bounds, but I wish I could say the same for my speaking. I had to go up to the local hospital once a week (Wednesdays') to see their Speech Therapist. My dad took me up there when he finished work. While I was out with my dad he used to encourage me to talk but as soon as we got back home my mum used to tell me to sit down and shut up because she was watching television. So I was even longer in the speech department, instead of being able to talk in about six months it took me about two years or longer in some cases.

It was the same with the physiotherapy I had to do at home, when I went to do my right leg, my right arm and hand exercises my mum used to tell me to stop as it was either dinner time or for some other reason. It was like every morning my mum used to push me in my wheelchair up the road to do the shopping. One morning I asked my mum if I could walk up there, she said 'No because she didn't have time to wait for me.' So I never asked again.

My friend Mel used to come round two or three times a week, after she finished work. She worked for the Post Office. We used to walk (I hobbled) down the road to look around the shops and we also popped into the local Social Services to see our friend Mark. He was a Senior Social Worker. He always had time to see us. We used to talk about anything and everything. Mark used to ask me questions and I tried my best to answer them. Mel used to walk with me to our secondary school. We used to go up there to see a few of the teachers. They were always pleased to see how well I was doing.

It was Christmas 1988 and I thought I had heard the last of Dick. When out of the blue he telephoned me. After he had finished speaking to me, I felt so sick inside because of the things he had done to me and the things he said. I have never told anyone about what had happened, as far as I was concerned that was in the past and it is the future I am looking for. Please let this be the last of what I am going to hear of him, that is my Christmas wish.

At the age of sixteen and three quarters I went to the local college on a one day per week scheme (Monday). When I went there I used to do a sort of English lesson in the morning and cooking in the afternoon. I went there for about six months. During the lunch breaks I sometimes met up with my best friend Sandy. I only saw her for about twenty minutes then I had to go because it took me about 15 minutes to walk to the huts I used to work in. I can remember doing a Dundee Cake that cost me £3.00. I can remember meeting a boy there, his name was Simon. He gave me his name and address; it was a place in Woking.

1989

At the age of seventeen I had to go into hospital up at Sheffield. It was a very large hospital, at least nineteen floors. At the time I had no idea why I was going to this hospital. I was to stay in this hospital for three nights and four days. My Uncle Ted took us (my mum, my dad, Kevin, my Nanny Hoy, Brandy and me) up to Sheffield in his car. We left early Monday morning, about 2am. We arrived there about 10 am. My Uncle Ted took my parents to a B&B, where they were going to stay before we went to the hospital.

When we got to the hospital we had to wait in the waiting room for about 30 minutes before I was taken to my bed. In the ward there were five women in the cubicle that I was to go into. I can only remember one, Dorothy. She was a middle aged woman, very slim with brown hair. The reason why I remember her was because she was the only one to speak to me. That evening she asked my mum for my address, my mum gave it to her and she gave my mum hers. I only stayed on this ward for two nights as they did the treatment in another part of the hospital. On the second day the doctor who was going to give me the treatment came up to the ward where my mum and dad were sitting with me. This doctor showed us where the treatment was going to happen. It was about five minutes walk away from the main part of the hospital (it took me about half an hour). When we got there we went into a building and got into a lift. Instead of going up we went down. I thought this is a bit strange. When we got out of the lift we went along a dull lighted corridor and into a room. In this room was a large looking machine. I was told that I had to have my head attached to a brace so they could give a direct radiation treatment to the affected areas. This machine had a large scanning trolley coming out of what looked like a bit helmet. At the time I didn't know what any of this meant. After the doctor showed us this machine, he took us back to the main hospital. Once we got there the doctor said that I was allowed to go out of the hospital with my parents, so we went out. We went around the shops and had something to eat out because the doctor said that I could. About 3 pm we went back to the hospital because I was feeling very tired.

The next day, Wednesday, I was not allowed any breakfast as I was to have my treatment. I was given two tablets (along with my normal medication) to make me drowsy. The next thing I remember was being slightly awake, and all these people in blue gowns around me. I felt a burning sensation around my groin. The next thing I remember was having these small screws drilled into my head, it was a brace being screwed to my skull, and it felt so heavy. The next thing I knew I was being pushed on this bed into an awaiting ambulance to take me to this other part of the hospital.

I arrived at the other part of the hospital in about five minutes. I was taken down to the basement where that machine was. The reason why I had the head brace on was because they had to screw my head into position so that they could get the right spots/brain haemorrhages were. This took about one hour. I can remember that someone said to me that I was about the thirty-third person in this hospital to have this treatment done.

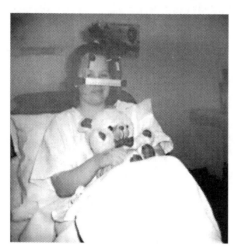

Head Brace and Machine
Wednesday 22nd February 1989
The Machine that did the final thing

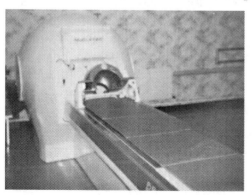

After this had taken place I was on my way up to the ward in this part of the hospital, when the lift door opened on the ground floor and my parents came into the lift as well. They said hello but I did not want them to see me in this state, but my parents did not listen to me. I was in a mess, where the head brace had been attached to my head/skull, I had bleed, and I had blood all down the back off my head, and had gone into my hair.

Later on when my parents left I still felt a little drowsy and I wanted to go to the toilet. I got out of bed with a struggle and out of the room I was in. I then asked a nurse where the toilet was, she quickly hurried over to me and said that I should not be out of bed. She helped me to the toilet, and then helped me back into bed. She then gave me the buzzer for next time I wanted something, and then left.

The following day I was discharged from the hospital. We made our way to the railway station, and then got on the train to Victoria, in London. On the train we had seats booked because it was a long journey. When we got there my dad went ahead to find my Uncle Frank, my Nanny Hoy and Kevin. My mum and I followed behind slowly. We then drove home, back to Addlestone. I went to bed as soon as I got in because I was very tired, as it had been a very stressful day.

The following day, I got out of bed and made my way down stairs. When I got down the bottom of the stairs I walked into the kitchen and said to my parents that my face was feeling all swollen and I feel sick. My mum said to me, go back to bed and it will be alright. So my dad helped me back upstairs and into my bed, where I soon fell asleep. A couple of days later, I found out that I had radiation treatment up at Sheffield and that was the only place in England that did this sort of treatment at that time.

A week or so later I felt fine. Mel came round to see how I was, and asked if I was ready to go out for our usual walk. I said yes, but my mum was a bit cautious about me going out but she let me go anyway.

As we walked up the road we took it nice and slowly. We decided to go and see our friend Mark. We were greeted like friends do. Mark asked me what I was going to do now that I have finished going to college. I said that I didn't know. He asked what my interests were. I said anything to do with office work. Then he had an idea about going to Egham Rehabilitation Centre. I said ok. So we filled in the form and sent them off.

A few days later I received a letter from the rehabilitation centre. It said that I had to go there for a week to see what sort of work they thought I would be good at. I showed Mark the letter and he was pleased that I got in so soon. My mum was not happy about me going to Egham as it was a residential place. Mark said that in some cases they do allow the person to travel there each day, and I would be one of those people.

It came to the day I went to Egham. I got up, washed and dressed ready to go. The taxi came and I went to the rehabilitation centre.

It was a large place, bigger than I expected. I had to wait in the reception for about ten to twenty minutes, I was not alone there were about five other people waiting there too. Eventually this gentleman came and introduced himself to us. He told us to follow him, so we all did. I did my best to keep up. We walked throw the work shop where other disabled people of all disabilities were working. In the bottom left hand of the work shop were two rooms and beyond that were some seats. We were shown to these seats and told to sit down. We were then taken one at a time and were given all these tasks to do. I did alright nearly all of them. The one I found difficult was having this machine that made coat hangers. I had difficulty in holding the strip of plastic and putting it round the pegs that were sticking out of the machine, but as the man said there are certain things people find easy and some hard. This lasted for four days, it was supposed to last for five days but we all finished the work early. After the course had finished I was sent another letter asking if I would like to go back for an eight week course to improve my skills, I said yes. I went back there in the October and that's when my life changed once again.

October came. I got the taxi to the rehabilitation centre, which I did every morning and it picked me up every evening, just because my mum would not let me stay there as residential. I think she didn't want to lose any money that is why she didn't want me to be residential. I managed to arrive there safely by taxi despite what the weather was like. I walked into the reception, and introduced myself to the man on reception. He told me to take a seat and someone would be along shortly. As I sat down I noticed someone else, it was a coloured woman. I can remember her name, Clara. We were both going to the same place of work. That was where they did office work, answering telephones etc. As we went into the large room, I noticed a young man working. We were shown to two desks and were talked to telling us what we were going to do over the next seven/eight weeks. As we were working that young man I noticed working came over and started talking to Clara, and then he turned to me and asked me what my name was. I said 'Joanna, but I prefer to be called Jo'. He said his name is David.

Later that day David went out of the room that we were in, then a few minutes later he came back in and came over to me. He said that they wanted me in the office along the corridor. So I went with him as I did not know where the office was so David had to show me. It was just along the corridor from the room where we were. I walked into the office behind David. Then, the ladies in the office said that they did not want me, so we walked back to the room. When we were out of the office David turned to me and said that he knew the ladies in the office did not want to see me, and that he wanted to get me alone to talk to me. I was taken back by this and did not know what to say. Instead I just walked (as fast as I could) back into the room with David following behind. I did not want David to see me blush. I don't know what the matter with me since I have suffered with my stroke I seemed to blush easily. And this was one of those occasions.

There was one afternoon when we had finished for the day. When we were going out of the room we had to clock out by putting a card with our names on it into a machine. I was just going out of the door when there was this young girl waiting for someone. This young girl had Down's syndrome; it was the first time I had ever come across anyone with this condition before. She asked me if David Barnes had come out yet. I replied that I didn't know, and carried on walking to catch my taxi home.

Over the few weeks David always spoke to me and I spoke back as best as I could. On David last day he asked me for my name and address, so I gave him it and he gave me his. This other fellow also asked me for my name and address. I felt so rotten afterwards but I gave him a made up address. I am so sorry but I did not like the look of this fellow.

The very next day I received a letter throw the post, I opened it. It was from David I couldn't believe it, someone writing to me. I took it with me to Egham and showed Clara. She was a bit jealous because she hadn't got one. I thought my luck must be on the up.

I soon sent a letter back, but as soon as I got that one in the post another one turned up. It seemed that for every one I posted two or three would arrive. I was beginning to get feed-up with all this, especially seeing as I didn't know what to say three quarters of the time, but I know one thing I did say was that if he wanted anything to come between us he had to give up smoking, and do you know what he gave up smoking just for me.

I have kept all my letters that David has sent to me and the same for I sent David. It's like I have kept most of my diaries since I have suffered a stroke. I even kept all the newspaper cuttings that concern me and my family.

Also in 1989, Mark (my social worker friend) offered me a job but he was not sure how much I was allowed to earn. So my mum phoned someone up that deals with finances and they said I was not allowed to earn anything but I could do it on voluntary bases. So my mum phoned Mark up and told him what the finance people had said. So I went to work the very next day for £15 per day. The work I did was to be doing with another woman was to be sorting out all the files out into categories, such as different dates, whether the person is blind or not, whether the person was a child being abused etc. But this job would not be starting until the New Year, which was fine with me.

1990

My 18ᵗʰ birthday.

It was my birthday on the 18th January, but I was having my 18th birthday party on the 6th. I was inviting allsorts of people, such as Mr Chambers (my form tutor from school), Simon (that boy I met from college), Timothy (an ex-boyfriend from secondary school), Mark and his partner (my social worker friend) and the rest was family. I did not invite David because I did not think he would be able to come. Timothy had a bit of an accident in one of the dances; he opened his legs a bit too much and split his trousers. Luckily enough we only live 5 minutes away so Stephen lent him a pair of his. For my birthday my Nan Hoy made me my birthday cake, the trouble was she made the icing so hard it was almost impossible for me to cut it.

I got 5 black bags of presents and cards, some of the cards had money in them too. Most of the presents I opened the next day they were jewellery. I also got chocolate a pair of slippers, and lots of other bits and pieces. Plus I still had my family's presents to come on the 18th, which I could not wait for.

My Nan Hoy and Uncle Ted took me out on the 17th to buy my birthday present. We looked round all the clothes stores until I saw a coat. It was a big rain mac. I was over the moon with it, but I did not see the price, but I know it roughly costs £90. But my Nan Hoy and Uncle Ted brought it for me. I was over the moon about it.

Today was the 18th, my birthday, I was 18 today. I was lucky to be here after what I had been through. Today I get the rest of my presents from the rest of my family. Of my Nan Norgate I got a jewellery box to put some of the jewellery in that I got from my birthday party. Of my Nan Hoy I got a typewriter which I was not expecting because of the coat, and a few other presents.

By now I was getting used to having to share Mel with Stephen seeing as they were falling in love with each other. One day she would come round for Stephen the next it would be for me, I would not know where I am with her spending all this time around here.

On the 30th January I started my first day of voluntary work with Mark (my social worker friend), we started by driving to pick up some cork for a notice board for his offices. Then we drove back to his offices to sort out what we were going to do about these files. I went to work twice a week to do the filing. I really enjoyed working with one of the ladies doing the filing.

David was still writing to me as often as before, infact he has started at the Queen Elizabeth Training College in Leatherhead for a short spell. I asked my mum if he could come for dinner one Sunday, she said yes. So I invited him to come on Sunday February 18th. I sat on the fence outside our place waiting for him to come, and he just walked straight pasted me, he didn't even recognize me. Not until I spoke to him and said, 'that's it just walk straight past'. And he said, 'Sorry I didn't even recognize you'. I took him in and introduce him to my parents and my brothers, they all liked him. Later on David and I went for a walk down to our local park and while we were out he became my boyfriend and I became his girlfriend. When we got back my dad said he would take David back to the college as it was a residential college.

On the 24th March we went to Guildford. We were going to go to Woking but my mum wanted to come along, so she went to Woking while we went to Guildford. When we got there it was drizzling with rain so we didn't hang about, we went straight to Argos. We went over to the ring cabinet and looked at them. David pointed one out to me and I said yes, they did it in my size too, J. He also looked at the earrings and picked out some crystal shaped hearts. After we had paid for these items we decided to go for something to eat in McDonalds, and it was there that David proposed to me and I said yes. A middle aged couple on the table next to ours overheard David propose to me and were the first people to say congratulations to us both, we said thank you to them both.

On the way home I felt a bit sick so we decided to get of the bus in Sheerwater, and sure enough once I got off the bus I was sick. We thought it was my travel sickness playing up and got on another bus a little while later. When we got home the first person we showed my ring to was my Nan Hoy, she was very pleased for us both. My mum was happy too, in her own way. We told my mum about me being sick she said it was probably my appendix playing up. She took me down to the local surgery the local doctor anyway, just to get it checked out. The local doctor said the same thing as my mum. So I went back home. Later that evening about 9.30pm I was rushed to hospital with appendicitis, they almost burst. I was in hospital for four days in all.

While all this was happening David was at college at Leatherhead worrying his mind out, the poor thing. He did visit me while I was in my local hospital. He got one of his student friend's to drive their car from the college over to the hospital just to visit me, wasn't that sweet. This trauma started David to smoke again, I could not blame him though, but I hope that he stops soon though.

My mum, my dad, my younger brother and I used to go over to Leatherhead to the Queen Elizabeth Training College so that I could see David, oh and so my mum could play their game of bingo. David used to call the numbers out because he used to do it for a local business in the town he comes from, Folkestone, Kent.

It was Thursday 12th April when David and I went down to Folkestone to visit David's flat. It is the first time I have ever been away from home by myself since my stroke. We arrived at 5 Harvey Place late in the evening so I did not get a look at the place, but it looked nice at what I could see. The next day, Friday 13th April, was a nice surprise for me; it was the day I lost my virginity on his living room floor. It was funny, David said 'Tell me if this hurts and I will stop'. I said 'Ouch that hurt, but try again'. And he did.

It was like on several trips down to Folkestone I had to spend several trips to William Harvey Hospital with concussion (as my head was very fragile at this time due to the radiation treatment I had the previous year) mostly due to the fault of David and his wicked sense of humour. The first time was both of our faults because we were both mucking about on the bed, he was tickling me I jumped back and banged my head against the bedroom wall and knocked my self out cold. The second time we were sitting face to face on the arm chair in his living room when I leant back to far and banged my head on the floor and knocked myself out cold. These are just two of many of the different cases that there are. They got to know me well up at the William Harvey Hospital.

There was David's Aunt Jenny and Uncle Roger who lives up Plain Road in Folkestone, with their Jack Russell dog named Wendy, who we often visited. I used to tease the dog, Wendy, with my chocolate biscuit by waving it about in the air before eating it, and this used to really torment her especially when in the end I ate it all and didn't give her a drop of chocolate. They are religious people and very much into music, any sort, I say any sort a part from heavy metal.

We even visited David's sister Chris, Phil & their family in Harlow, Essex. One particular time we went there to house sit and to look after their dog. We were sleeping in their double bed when we heard them leave; as we heard the door shut David decided he wanted his breakfast, not the food kind of breakfast but the sexual type of breakfast. Unknown to us Chris had come back in for her passports; she forgot that they were in her bedside cabinet. She came in and David was still down there, she just laughed and I went bright red with embarrassment, while David just stayed under cover. Chris told the rest of the family and we got taken the micky out of from the rest of the family when we came back home.

On our visit down to his flat we also visited an old lady, Margaret. She was a nice lady while David was at home she had him there doing odd jobs about the home for her, like paint all her up-stairs for her because she had not been up there for years. To me she was like a third Grandmother. You see she had no children of her own because she never got married because she spent all her life in service, even when she got old she carried on working. I often did her dusting for her and I had to put things back exactly where they came from, that was one of the things she learnt when she worked. We also met his Aunt Jenny and Uncle Roger there because they popped in there for their tea. They are a nice couple.

One of David's closest friend's was Victor Smith, he was a gay man, that did not both us because we found that the gayer the friend the truer they are. And that is true. Victor had just met another gay man, Raymond, who he is very fond off, even though he is a few months older than me and Victor is a lot older than we are, but who's counting as long as they are happy, now that counts.

We spent quite a few weekend breaks down at Folkestone. My mum, my dad and Kevin used to come down on the Sundays', just for the day though. Sometimes my Nan Hoy and Uncle Ted used to come down too, because my Uncle Ted used to get free tickets because he used to work for British Railway.

On the 3rd August David and I were going down to Folkestone to spend a fortnight down there because David was due to do to his work experience at the local newspaper place.

On the 7th August we phoned my mum up from David's and she suggested that I phoned Dick (from the Wolfson Centre) up, because he lived in Dymchurch, that was just down the road from Folkestone. We phoned Dick up; little did David know about the time before in the hospital or about the phone call that Christmas. We arranged to meet up together on the Thursday evening, the 9th as David had his work experience during the day. I thought I would be safe with David by my side.

On the 9th August David left at 9am to go for his work experence. At 9.30am the buzzer went on the intercom, I thought it was David; but he would have used his key, but instead it was Dick. Like anyone would have done, I let him in. He came up. I opened the door and let him in. He was a large man in size and in build. He had a big beard that made him look like a builder. As he came in he sat down on the stall next to the breakfast bar. I asked him if he would like a drink. He replied 'yes a cup of coffee'. So I made him a cup of coffee like he requested. I then sat on the arm of the arm chair. Dick then said 'How about a kiss to say hello then'. So I gave him a kiss on one of hairy cheeks, just to say hello, then I went to sit down but he wouldn't let me go. Instead he put his left arm around me so I could not move. With his right arm he managed to get my top of me and take my bra down my waist. He then started to kiss my left breast and the started to bite my left breast. The more I tried to get away the more he held on. Then to my relieve David came in and Dick let go. I ran past David; into the bed room. I heard David say to Dick 'I think you had better go'. And with that Dick left. David came into the bed room.

In the bed room David asked me if I was alright, I said no. He told me to stay where I was because he was going to call the police. He was gone just ten minutes. They arrived just ten minutes after. It was two police women that came. They told me to tell them everything that had happened. So I told them everything, even what had happened two years previous. David was shocked, he had no idea what had happened before. The police women were there for about two hours, writing down everything. They then left saying that someone would be round Dick's house as soon as possible.

They also suggested that David took me to see his doctor to get me checked out for bruising around the left breast. So David took me to see his local doctor. While we were in his waiting room David notice a number on his notice board and got up and asked the receptionist if she had a pen and paper he could borrow, she gave them to him. He wrote down something, I am not sure what. Anyway it was time for us to go into see the doctor. David told the doctor what had happened, then the doctor turned to me. He asked me if I minded if he touched my breast. I said 'I did not mind', because I knew David was there. The doctor said that there was some bruising around the teeth marks but apart from that nothing to serious. David said about me sleeping tonight, would I have problems? I said 'yes, I would.' So the doctor gave me some very weak sleeping tablets. After that we left.

That left me in a bit of a mess. I didn't know what to do with myself. I couldn't stay in that flat. He took me to a bench that was near a phone box and told me to sit there, which I did. While he went to the phone box and phoned someone. All he told me when he got back was that some one was coming shortly to help me, and sure enough in about 30 minutes time someone came.

This tall thin man, with a beard and long blonde hair came walking up to us and held out his hand and said 'hello, my name is Anthony.' Anthony then asked if there was anyway we could talk. David said that there was his flat just round the corner, I quickly said no, because I didn't want to go back to that flat. So David said hang on I will just phone my Aunt and see if we can go up there. That left me alone with Anthony for a few minutes, and Anthony started talking but before I could answer David came back with good news his Aunt's place was going to be empty for the evening so we have got all evening to chat.

So Anthony drove us up to Aunt Jenny's place, which is a lovely place. As you come in the front door is the main bedroom, the turn right walk along the corridor, the first door on the right is the bathroom, you carry on walking on you come to the living room/ dinning room, you go to the door it the door it the top right hand corner and you come to the kitchen, in the kitchen you go through the door and you come to another bedroom. That's the ground floor. Upstairs there are two other bedrooms and another shower and toilet. Plus another complete flat, this is rented out.

Back to when Anthony came to visit. He drove all the way up to where Aunt Jenny lived. When we went into her house we were greeted by her Jack Russell, Wendy. David went off into the kitchen to make us all a cup of tea while Anthony and I sat down and began to chat. I began to tell Anthony about Dick and what had happened, he listened to it all. We were there for about two and a half hours. After all the chat we had come to the conclusion that we were going back to David flat.

David went in first then I went in followed by Anthony. The cup of coffee I had made Richard was still in the cup. It had gone cold; the milk had gone cold on top of it. David got hold of the cup and tipped the contents away, and threw the cup away; it was one of David's favourite cups. Anthony asked if I had his name and address in my address book, I replied yes. So I got my name and address book, and turned to his name and address. Anthony then asked if I had anyone else's name and address I wanted to save. I said yes, so I copied down their name and addresses. After that Anthony tore out Dick's name and address and I watch him burn it. We did a bit more talking, and we decided to go over to Lydd, to where David's mother, Joan and step-father, Ron lived. Anthony said that he would take us, and we said thank you.

Over at Lydd, David A.B. phoned my mum up to tell her what had happened. I would not speak to her as I did not talk to anyone because I felt so guilty for what had happened, I felt it was my fault, I felt as though I let him do it to me. I felt so ashamed for what had happened. When in fact none of it was my fault at all, I did not let him do this to me he helped him self, he forced his way into my space, my private space. It took a couple of days before I spoke to my mum; she was all sympathetic, which is unusual for my mum.

I spent quite a few times in the William Harvey Hospital, Ashford Kent, this year that the nurses in casualty seem to know me by sight rather than by name.

I came down to David's flat quite a few times since that incident. On one occasion David went out and brought two tickets to see Des O'Conner at the Leas Cliff Halls, Folkestone. Neither of us had seen him before, so it would have been a surprise for both of us.

We enjoyed the show a great deal; I would recommend his show to anyone. After the show had finished David had arranged it for us to see Des behind the stage. I couldn't believe my luck, and to go with it Des gave me a red rose and he gave me three kisses on the left cheek; but before he did he asked if it was alright if he could because David had let them know before about the incident that had happened. We had a late night that night, about 1am, so we had a late morning the next day.

1991

On February 6th was the court case about the assault. It was held at Maidstone Crown Court. It was beautiful inside with a magnificent marble stair case leading up to the courts. We were led by someone who works with the ushers who took us to where the police offices wait until they are called. We were there forever, but my mum went ahead to the court room to listen to what was happening. She was gone for a long time. About 3 hours later we were taken to the court room and told that the court had come to a verdict, even without me giving evidence. I wondered why I was not allowed to give any evidence, it was all due to my mum, she must have given some evidence against me like saying that I was in no fit state to give any evidence or something like that. Anyway the court had given a verdict, which was he could be bound over to keep the peace for a year, and if not he had to pay £350 fin. Whatever it was, it was not enough, he should have got a sentence, if anything. After the court case, as we came walking out of the court the barrister who was defending me came over to me and shock me hand saying how brave I am to face everyone like that. I didn't know what to say, so I didn't say anything and just shook his hand and smiled.

On Friday 8th February it took us from 2pm, that is the time we left Folkestone, and the time my Uncle Ted picked us up was 8pm. It normally takes us about 3 hours in stead it took us double that, because of the snow. It was very bad snow, because of the snow the trains some of them were cancelled, that is why it took us so long. It was the first time I had ever had seen it snow in February, I had only ever seen it snow in November, December and January before.

The reason why we had to come home on the 8th is because Stephen and Mel were getting married tomorrow (on the 9th). And my mum had brought a summery dress to wear in all that snow and to top that she was wearing a pair on sandals. I bet she was freezing. The vicar that married Stephen to Mel was one of Mel's form tutors back in 1984/5; he was also an old geography teacher of mine. The wedding went off fine. We stood out in the snow having our photos taken. My mum was freezing to death in her brand new summers dress. I was wearing a blue suit I had brought in Woking market.

On the 13th February I had to go up to Adkinson Morley Hospital for an Angiogram. This is where they put a die in throw the groin and watch it go around the brain/heart. There is a 5% chance that epilepsy will develop. And guess what I took that 5% chance, I developed epilepsy. David came and visited me in hospital while I was in here, which was nice. I had an epileptic fit whilst he was visiting, but that did not put him of me, which I was glad. I only stayed in there for a few days, and then I was an allowed home.

David and I were going to live together but my mum would not let us, she said the only way you are going to live together is if you get married. So we said fine, and went down to St Paul's Church in Addlestone, Surrey and arranged a date for us to get married which would be on Saturday 22nd June 1991. This was only three months away. My mum said that she would love to make my wedding dress. So I said ok, but I would choose the pattern. This was alright with my mum. So the following day we went out to buy the material, cotton and bits and pieces. Instead of having a bouquet of flowers for me as I suffer with hay fever my mum was going to make a heart shaped cushion with my name and David's name on it with the date we got married on it. She was also going to make something smaller for the bridesmaids as well.

We had to decide who to choose who were to be our bridesmaids. There were my cousins, Sophie and Annabell, my friend from school, Caroline. That was on my side. On David side there was his niece, Mandy, and Sally (the Down's syndrome girl I mentioned earlier). That left an odd one we decided to ask Margaret, because she had never been married before and it was her biggest dream to be a bridesmaid, so we asked her, and she said yes. So that made the six. We have told all the families concerned except Sally's; that they would have to buy their own dresses; we are going for tea tomorrow we will ask her then.

Today we are going to visit Sally and her family; we are not expected there until 5pm so we went round to the park. It was a beautiful sunny day, so we sat on the bench for a while. When it was time we went round there we went round to their house, it was a large house. We went through into the living room throw into the garden where Sally was sitting in a large garden. We went up to Sally and said hello. We started talking, that's when David mentioned about

Sally being one of our bridesmaids. Sally said she would love to, but she would have to buy her own dress. She asked what colour it would have to be, we said pink.

A couple of months before we got married David went down to the flats in Hythe, Kent, that were in Sir John Moore Avenue, to set up our things in our new flat. It was a nice flat, it was a purpose built flat for a disabled person, so that everything was a level height for a person in a wheelchair. David had already started to make friends with some of the neighbours; two of them are Judy and Brian, they were very nice people. I used to call Brain 'my little honey bunch', mind you there were a few people I used to call my little honey bunch.

It came to the night before my wedding; I am supposed to have my hen night. It was alright I suppose my mum, my Nan Hoy, my sister-in-law Mel, Caroline and Sandy were there. They all had an alcoholic drink except for my mum who only day diet coke and I of course me I had pineapple juice. We had a good laugh about one thing and another. The only thing was we all went home by 10 o'clock at night. I was soba what a bore.

My wedding day. I got up at my usual time because today was going to be a busy day for everyone. Later on this morning I was going to the hairdressers to get my hair done ready for this afternoon at 4.30pm when I was due to walk down the isle. It must have been about 2pm when I received a phone call from Simon (the Boy I met from college), he asked what I was doing, and I replied getting ready for my wedding at 4.30 this afternoon. And with that he quickly hung up, I don't know why? I think he must have phoned me up to ask me out for a date or something like that. What a shame I will never know.

I had already asked my Uncle Harry if he could drive my dad and me to the church, and he agreed. He had already dropped my Aunty June and my cousin Annabell off at the church. My cousin Sophie could not make it as she had a brownies/guides camp to go to instead. Anyway back to my wedding. My Uncle Harry drove us to the church for 4.30pm. We were a few minutes late but that was expected, seeing I was still in the wheelchair. We made sure all the bridesmaids had their hearts were ready to walk down the isle. But to everyone surprise, I walked from the car and down the isle, but the wheelchair was waiting for me at the altar with a chair next to it for David to sit in. We said our vows, missing out the bit about having children, because I cannot have children; which the vicar knew about.

The wedding went perfectly, except David real father did not turn up so his Step-father Ron stepped in and signed the wedding certificate along with my dad. David real father turned up for the reception, a bit late, but as they say 'better late than never'. The wedding ceremony took half an hour, and when that finished I

managed to walk out holding on to David arm. Passing my Nan Norgate (on the way out) she passed me a cheque for £100; she was not talking to my mum at that moment so she did not come to the reception, which was a shame but that was between my mum and my Nan.

The reception went alright to start with. It was held at the local pub (it has been pulled down now) The Dukes Head. We were the first ones to arrive there, but were shortly followed. As people arrived they put envelopes into a wishing well which was by the door. The best man, David Uncle Roger, made sure everyone had a drink as it was time to make the speeches, and sure enough Roger did. We gave out our crosses for the Brides maids and our gift for our best man. We also gave our cross to my third gran Margaret; I said I would treat her like a Brides maid. After that the music started and the rain started to show it self.

About an hour though I decided to go home and get changed so Roger took me and Caroline back to my mum and dad's so that I could get to get changed. Roger said that he would wait in the car, while Caroline would come inside with me. I changed in to a pair of trousers and a stripped shirt. It took me about 15 minutes, after that Roger took us back to the reception.

Our reception was different we did not have presents because we had all the essential things' like: towels, tea towel, clocks, knifes/forks, sauce pans etc. The only thing we really needed was a double bed. So we had a wishing well, and we got about £700 which was a lot in 1991. The wedding and reception only cost us £250 that was a lot of money in 1991.

As I mentioned before the reception started of fine. I was going round all the guests one at a time, when I got to my second cousin Freddie and his wife Sue. When Freddie offered to buy me a drink, I agreed, and went with him to the bar. On the way back, I passed my drink down to Sue and went to step down to her level when I stepped down to far fell back and knocked myself out cold. An ambulance was called. In the ambulance the ambulance driver had to ask the directions to the hospital. David had to say that he did not know himself because he was new to area himself.

When we got to the hospital I had come round. The hospital staff had decided to keep me in over night. David's sister Chris came up the hospital because her youngest daughter Mandy (one of our brides maids), wanted to see me, to make sure I was alright. Later that night David A.B. slept next to me in the hospital, so you could say I was the one that said 'not to night Josephine', because I had the headache.

The next day (Sunday 23rd June 1991) our friend of the family Molly, came with my Dad to pick us up from the hospital and take us home to Hythe in Kent. My mum could not come with us because she could not fit in Molly's mini. We left after dinner so we got there about 4ish.

David had been to our flat before and set things out, the only thing missing was a double bed but in its place were two single beds. My dad and Molly did not stay long as Molly had to be up early next morning to open the paper shop, and my dad had to be up early to do his milk round.

A few weeks later my dad, my brother Stephen and his new wife Mel came down with all my belongings (my clothes, my dressing tables, my wardrobe and all my soft toys).

In July, August and September 1991 David took driving lessons, and in September he took his driving test and passed. I was well pleased with him; all he had to do now was to find a car that we could afford. David looked in the papers. And there was one, a ford escort mark 2 for £350; it was a V reg (an old V reg). We went to have a look at it, the spare wheel was the original wheel that had never been used, and the car was in good condition. So we brought it there and then.

We only had that car for six months before some old woman crashed into us and the car was a right off. Luckily I was not in the car at the time, I was in the hospital.

I spent a lot of time in hospital because of my epilepsy, mainly causing problems in the evening or during the night time. Mind you there was one time in December 1991 when I went into hospital for an operation, this was to be sterilised. This time people are supposed to stay in for this operation two days but because of my medical history I was told to stay in there for 4 days at least.

It was at the beginning of 1992 that we had a phone call from David's real Father saying help I am in trouble with the police. Can you come and get me.

What were we supposed to do but go and get his Father? So we hired a Bluebird car and went up to Oxford. When we got up there his Father was just going to go into court, not for sentencing but just for a hearing. I was told to wait outside because I was in a wheelchair and there were steps leading up to the courtroom. David went ahead because he wanted to see what his Father was being charged for. After the court case had been heard David came back to me.

After the court case had been heard David's Father had been released on bail. So that meant that he could come home with us. He was due to be back in court the following week. When he came home with us, David and himself went into Folkestone, Kent to his father's bank and arranged it so that David could withdraw money on his father's behalf. There was about £20.000 in there. So by the time they came home David was an executor for his father.

It had been three days since David's Father had been with us when there had been a knock at the door, it was the police. There had been an incident in Folkestone and they had pointed the finger straight away at David's Father. Just because he was new to the area they automatically thought it was David's Father. So they arrested David's Father even though we said that he had been with us all the time.

The day of the court case, David's Aunt Jenny came with us because she came with us in a van to clear his Father's flat out. We went to the court first to hear how long he had got, 6 years. It was not to long because he gave himself up, instead of them finding him out. After the court case we went to his flat, the trouble was we didn't have his keys, so we had to call the police to break into his flat. They came and they made a good job of breaking the door frame, but never mind it's only a policeman doing his job.

Once we got into his flat we took all his belongings down to the van. We decided to take most of the furniture: the wardrobe, the wall units from the front room. We decided to leave the settee and armchair, as they were too big. We took all the pictures down off the walls, so he had plenty of pictures to hang up when he got out of prison into his own place.

David's father had so much stuff, almost enough stuff to start again if he wanted to. In the end David and I have said that he could live with us when he comes out of prison, that is if he wants to or not?

1992

By this time we had got in touch with mobility about getting a car and they accepted our claim. We chose a red mini metre whose registration number plate was J719 MKL and because it was nice and compact, just what we needed.

It was early January and we had just been up visiting my parent's when my epilepsy took hold of me. It was a session of grand mull ones with the arching back. Luckily for David we were just coming past Maidstone, Kent so we went straight into the hospital there. As soon as I was taken in I was taken up to Intensive Care because as soon as I was coming out of one fit I was going back in to another. So I don't remember the first few days. After that, when I was taken down to the wards, I was taken down to the mixed wards. It was nice, there was this tall male nurse called Steve, he was 6 foot 6 inches tall with blonde hair.

Now in this mixed ward, I liked it, I made friends with this male patient next to me. He was in because he had a heart attack when he was driving his lorry. I liked to watch his heart monitor as it went across each time, and he used to watch out for me each time I used to have a fit.

While I was in Maidstone I had an appointment to see a consultant in the William Harvey Hospital, Ashford, Kent, which was just down the road from Maidstone. So as not to make things complicated Maidstone arranged for an ambulance to take me to the William Harvey Hospital. On the trip between the two hospitals I had 7 fits. The ambulance crew and a nurse (a temp nurse) wheeled me in to see the consultant while I was having a fit. So what does the consultant do but have a go at the ambulance crew for bring me, then has a go at the nurse for not being the proper nurse. Then turns to me, David says that you only have to tap to tap her on the forehead to knock her out, so what does the consultant do but taps hard on my forehead.

After the ambulance crew and nurse had come out of there, they all said that they would put that in a report about the consultant and that they hope that David would too. Later that day, a consultant from the Maidstone Hospital came to see us. He heard about what had happened with the other consultant and wanted to offer his services, we accepted.

I had some bad news while I was in Maidstone Hospital. It was that my third Grand Mother Margaret had died. It is a shame but I look at it like at least we filled her biggest dream of becoming a brides maids. My mum came down for Margaret's funeral; it was held in the church in Folkestone, none of her family arranged her funeral David's Aunt Jenny did all the arrangements as at the time Margaret was living at her home.

David gave me a surprise, he wrote off to Des O'Conner to get a signed autograph for me. Wasn't that nice of him? I still have that autograph but the writing has faded, I would love to get another one someday but who knows when?

A few months later, our friend Liz came down to stay with us for a short time. I met her when she went to the Queen Elizabeth Training College in Leatherhead, Surrey and she was friends with David. I liked her but I don't like her, if you know what I mean. She also suffers from epilepsy but hers' are on a different level to mine.

When she stayed with us for a short time, this time my epilepsy was at its worst. There was one evening about 10 pm; I awoke to find David not in bed beside me but to find him in the living room with Liz lying on the put-you-up bed top less and David was massaging her. I walk-in not looking at them, and walk-in over towards the fridge to get a glass of orange juice, I then turned round and walked straight out not looking at what they are doing. David got up and followed me into the bedroom mumbling something; I was not listening to what he was saying; so I just said 'ok darling, I want to go to sleep now'. So he went back to the living room to clear his things away. I never did find out what he did say that night.

A couple of mornings later I was having a lazy morning in bed, when David and Liz decided to come and join me. David and I had talked about have a three some in bed, but never actually done it, that is until now. Well I must admit I never dreamed it would be anything like this before, it certainly was an experience. We only did it the once, I think we were a disappointment for Liz, we were not up to her standard. I was only I beginner at this sort of thing, I mean what does she expect, it to be handed to her on a gold plate.

My epilepsy was still playing up as much as last year, but that did not stop me from joining a disabled swimming club once a week. They taught me to swim using an arm band on my right arm and using my left arm and left leg. I can swim better than David can and he swims normally. We do this once a week. For instance, one week in Folkestone swimming pool I swam their main pool 15 times while David only managed to swim it 6 times.

The swimming club committee had their annual meeting and once a year they choose a couple to go away on holiday to Great Yarmouth, and they chose David and me. What a shock. The reason why they decided to pick us is because we never had a honeymoon, so this was a late honeymoon. And we enjoyed ourselves especially when I entered him for the Knobbly Knees contest and he got his own back when he entered me for the judges. Even on this holiday my epilepsy comes with me, but David managed to cope with it by himself.

While we were in Great Yarmouth we got some of those naughty stickers you put on the back window of the car. One of them said 'Me not silly, me wear condom on my willy'. Now that is not too bad, is it? Well there were some of the residents around Sir John Moore Avenue that could not take a joke, so they got in contact with the local councillor, who got in contact with us. David said if they don't like it they can talk to us nicely instead of sending rude comments across the path. A couple of days later David was out and there was a phone call, I took it. It was this councillor and he said I see you have not removed to stickers yet? And I said 'the car is in my name and as far as I am concerned the stickers are staying', and with that hung up. After that I was shaking, after all it is not every day I say things like that to a councillor.

In the summer we had one of David's nieces' staying with us. We had been swimming in Folkestone and were on our way back to our flat, when a Brigadier pulled out of the council offices in Hythe, Kent and smacked straight into the side of us. It frightened our niece but apart from that she was aright. Me, it made me bang my head against the side of my door and made me have terrific epileptic fits. The police were called and they got rid of the Brigadier before they called for the doctor to see to me. As they watched the Brigadier back they had to bang on the back of his car because he backed into the side of the police car.

Doctor Foster (our doctor at that particular time) came along as it was only across the road from the surgery. He gave me some injections but they did not seem to work so he suggested calling for an ambulance. The ambulance took 15 minutes to arrive. By this time the Brigadier was well out of sight.

When the ambulance got to the hospital, I was just coming round. My husband, who was David, came round the curtain, I did not recognize him, and I did not know who anyone was. Not even my mum and dad.

The hospital even released me even though I did not know who I was or where I was going. David assured them and me that I was in safe hands. When we got to what we called home David telephoned my mum and told her what had happened. Between the two of them they arranged a meeting for the Sunday (today being Wednesday).

On the Sunday my mum, my dad, my brother Kevin and my friend Caroline (one of my brides' maids) came down to visit me. Ready to jog my memory, but they did not succeed, not even a little bit. But what they have told me is what I have told you so far, so if they have been telling the truth or lies, lays on them and what they have told me.

One thing I do remember is that David's two cousins used to come down to our flat in Sir John Moore Ave, Hythe, Kent. We used to go down to the local pub in the evenings. I can remember one particular time we all had our usual non-alcoholic larger and non-alcoholic wine for me. Anyway, we were all walking back, when I couldn't walk anymore. So David and his cousins decided to carry me. If anyone had watched us they would have died laughing because it was a sight for sore eyes.

My epilepsy was being a real pain this year, for instance, it was a very wet late night when my epilepsy started up. I had grand mall serious, I was fitting like a trouper. The ambulance came to our flat, Sir John Moore Avenue; Hythe in Kent, instead of parking in the car park, the ambulance came right up on the path and spoiled some of the plants. Some of the neighbours' complained about it, don't worry about me just worry about the stupid plants.

It was November and I was in Buckland Hospital in Dover following a spell of epileptic fits. The cubical I was in was diabolical there was blood stains on the curtains and up the walls, in the locker there was a mouldy orange and a full bottle of laxative tablets. It was disgusting, you would have thought there would have been a cleaner to clean these things, but was not there was only a cleaner to clean the floors.

While I was in there I counted the number of tablets I had to take a day, 24 in all. No wonder I was more like a zombie not knowing what day was what which.

I came out of hospital on the Wednesday and on the Friday I said to myself right I am not taking anymore tablets, and put them on one side and did not touch them anymore. And do you know I have felt 100% better since.

1993

Meanwhile, David was having a spending spree with his Father's money, who he had control of because his Father had signed all his money over to him while he was in prison. It was as if it was like his father owed him the money from all the years he did not know him. We did visit him when he sent a visiting order form to see him.

I am still off my tablets and it is coming up to my 21st birthday and I am having a birthday party. David asked the hospital if they could do the food for my 21st birthday party and they replied yes. The food was wonderful there was enough there to feed an army. The birthday cake was lovely. It was chocolate sponge with white icing with the picture of a young girl on it.

We had invited my mum, dad my younger brother. We had also invited my friend Caroline (who was my brides' maid), the members of the swimming club, and some members of David's family. I totally enjoyed myself. My mum felt a bit left out, so David gave her the job of cutting the cake up. That kept her quiet. The music which was hired was a duet. We held a raffle and raffled off some large soft toys, my mum got a soft dog and there were four other prizes to go. We raised something like £45 in all, which was not bad. At the end of the evening there was so much food left over that everyone took a dish full home.

A fortnight later we were moving out of this flat into a flat on the sea front, Pensand House, South Road, Hythe, Kent. David's brother George lives in the flat opposite. George was living with his common-law wife Mildred, and once a fortnight he had one of his sons' Dan come to stay for the weekend.

Once a week David used to go to the Victoria Hospital, Folkestone to do an hour of fitness with Jack Bryan, I used to go and read a book or to watch David A.B.

One Wednesday I stayed at home and David brought one of the other men home with him, his name was Paul and he was about 6 foot tall with brown hair with grey bits in it. That was due to old age, he was 45. We both said to him that he could come up any time he wanted because we would be in any time. He said thank you and he would accept our offer.

David got himself a voluntary job in driving, sometime he would be out from 9.30am in the morning until 4pm in the afternoon. I would not mind but it left me all alone with no-one to talk to, nothing to do after I had done the house work, that is until Paul came in to play.

It started off on this summers' day when David had gone out early and would be out until about 5pm that evening. I had done all the hovering and dusting, made our bed and tided the kitchen, actually done everything. It was about 12 noon and there was a knock at the door, I answered it, it was Paul. He came in. We had a sandwich and a chat in the front room. Then it started, Paul came over to where I was sitting and we started kissing. Then we started, Paul pulling his shorts' down and me pulling my skirt up and my knickers' down. Then he stuck it inside of me, it felt so good. In out in out, the feeling, now I know what the feeling of a real man feels like. Paul would not come inside me, I don't know why; perhaps it was something he just did not want to do or something like that.

Another time we were on the way to Canterbury, Kent when we stopped in a field. Paul got a blanket out of the car and laid it on the ground, we got on top. On top of the blanket we made love, he ended up with no clothes on and he end-up with taking all my clothes off too. We end up kissing and doing David's favourite number, number 69, in case you don't know what one of these is I will tell you. A 69 is where a man and a woman go head and foot, then the man and woman lick or suck the private part.

Another time was in Folkestone, Kent we were up at the Leas. I was wearing a skirt with no knickers' and a t-shirt, and we were walking along the Leas when we came along a bench, were we sat down, me on top of him and started kissing and cuddling. We did this for about half an hour, then I stopped because I noticed a couple who had been sitting on the bench next to us had been giving us dirty looks. So we stopped and got up and walked off towards Paul's car. When we got there we drove off up to Paul's home because his wife had heard so much about me that she wanted to meet me. I felt so guilty about meeting her and have this affair with her husband, it just did not fill right, and then there were their two children.

One morning David went out and Paul phoned and said it's no good he has to be with me for ever. I was shocked, I had no idea it would be like this, but I agreed to be with him.

I waited for David to come back and the way I acted by not letting him kiss me or cuddle me he knew something was wrong. He asked and asked and finally I told him. He took me keys off me so I could not unlock the front door. He went out of the front door and locked it after him. He went next door to get his brother George, who came in and called me all the names under the sun. Meanwhile, Paul had turned up down below and I was shouting to him from our flat bedroom window.

David had called for a police officer to come because he did not want me to go, but the way I was feeling I wanted to go. The police officer let me go, and Paul welcome me with open arms.

We went to Paul's home, little did we know that David had already phoned up there to let Paul's wife know what had happened. Once we got there Paul went in first and I heard all the names under the sun insinuated at me, so I turned round and headed for the car. About ten minutes later Paul came out with a bag of clothes. We made our way towards Maidstone; we were going to go up to Paul's parents place, where ever that is.

We stopped half way at the car park, where Paul got out of the car so I got out of the car. We saw this other fellow so Paul started to follow him, holding my hand I followed behind. We saw that this man climbed over this tree that had fallen across a path way covering a little pocket, so that nobody could see in unless you knew you were there. Anyway, the three of us were in this pocket and I was the only female in there and there were two males, you can guess what was going to happen, can't you? I didn't have much choice in the matter, I couldn't really say no, could I? At least I did not let either of them come inside of me, I was too proud to let them try, after all I was David and I had married him.

When we got to Maidstone we stopped the car, we both had a thought and a chat, and come to the conclusion that we should go back home. There was a phone box across the road and we went across there to phone our partners to ask for forgiveness. We tried David first there was no answer, so we tried his mum, she said go to her place. Now it was time to try his wife. I did try to apologise but she just gave me a load of verbal abuse back which I could not blame her. So I just gave to phone back to Steve1, and went back to the car, he followed in about 5-10 minutes later.

Steve1 drove me to David mum, Joan's house in Lydd, Kent. When we got there he got my bag out of the boot of his car, and while he gave it to me he said how sorry he was and he hoped that we could still be friends. I said that maybe we could, but in the back of my mind there was a bit of hate building up. He also said that he had organised a sponsored run around the Radner Park, Folkestone, Kent on their Donkey Derby Day and perhaps we could go down there. I said maybe.

Inside Joan's place we sat in the kitchen and talked, well I mainly listened to what she had to say. Then she asked why I did it? And I answered that I did it because David had left me alone for hours and hours, and I just wanted company. Joan said she could see it from both points of view, but wait for David to come and the two of us have a chat and see where things go from there.

About an hour later David turned up in our car with his brother George and his common law wife, Mildred. George and Mildred were doing some odd jobs around their Nan's house, two doors down from their mum's. Meanwhile, David and I went for a walk to talk things through. We must have walked for about an hour or so, we both did some talking. David said sorry for not being there when he was needed and I said that was alright, I could have gone around George and Mildred's. In fact that's what I will do in future.

After we had finished our talk we had decided to try again. On the way home George and Mildred never said a word to me, come to think of it they never said a word to David either, I wonder why!

The next morning I woke up with the sound of the sea lapping up against the beach, it was beautiful. I soon got up. David was in the kitchen making breakfast. He asked what shall we do today, I said about the Donkey Derby Day, and that Paul was doing a sponsored run around Radner Park, Folkestone. David face lightened up as if he was up to mischief, but what could he do.

When we got there it was packed out with people, of all shapes and sizes. In the middle of the green was the donkeys all lined up ready for the derby. There was a man taking money for the bets. And on the outskirts, was the lads, running for the sponsors. On one corner was Paul, we never went over to him, instead we stood on the opposite corner. We only stayed there for about half an hour then we left.

After that we heard nothing from Steve1 or any of his family. That did not both me and I know that it certainly did not both David.

Later in the year we went to pick up Liz from the YMCA, because she was staying in one of their apartments. Liz came down to stay for a week or so. We were doing fine until she did something that did not agree with the both of us, so we told Liz she had to go. She said she would go by bus, so she had to walk across the green before she came to the main road, whatever way she went we could see her from our window.

We waited and waited but no Liz was sighted. We waited for 40 minutes but still no sight of her, but by this time there was a knock at the door. It was Liz being helped up be a middle aged man, who said that she was found having a fit down by the road side. That is why we could not see her, because she was having a fit by the road, typical. David helped her in, he said that this still does not change things she still going back but this time he was driving her back there himself. And he did.

Our friend Victor Smith and his partner Raymond had just lost their dog, they had to have him put down, due to old age. So they have just got themselves a Jack Russell and named her Tammy. They brought her up to our flat and she is so sweet. I wish they would stay that sweet all the time, but they all grow up sooner or later.

Living in this flat is like living in a draft box, every time we had wind the carpets waved with the wind. We had to keep the plugs in the plug holes because we got drafts through them. When we sat on the toilet set you rocked from side to side. The frame on the bedroom door came out because it was not screwed to the wall. The cupboard in the kitchen was not fixed to the wall so when you went to put things in to it, it came away from the wall. And finally there was a hole in the floor in the corner of the floor in the spare room.

The only things of these that were sorted out were the frame on the door, and the cupboard in the kitchen. The rest we're still waiting to be done. It is like David brother George's flat next door, his place is just the same. His carpets are the same as ours; it is the same with the plugs. Now have you ever heard of opening windows by taking the whole window out, window frame and all, well they did.

One morning David woke up with terrible pain in his neck, he just put it down to sleeping awkwardly, I agreed with him. As the day went on the pain got worse and worse, so David suggested that he would go up to the hospital to get it checked out, I said that I would go with him but I wanted to watch a programme on telly first. When we got down to the hospital they said that David had to where a collar because he had sprained his neck; but to make sure he was to go to the fracture clinic during the week.

At the fracture clinic they said to David 'Have you ever had it x-rayed'. David said no. So they x-rayed it and it showed a fracture mark across his neck. He had actually broken his neck, yet all the things he has done throughout his life and yet he had broken his neck. No wonder the poor thing was in so much pain. The hospital gave him another collar and some strong pain killers and said that they would inform our local doctor by letter.

1994

In the spring of this year I started at college in Folkestone, Kent. I started doing a NVQ Office Practice course level 1, it was supposed to be a 6 week course, but because I was the only disabled person on the course I was allowed to do the next 6 week course, so in fact I did 12 weeks instead. And because I was doing 12 weeks I was allowed to do parts of NVQ Office Practice course level 2. I only did 2 parts of level 2, and they were Finance and Word Processing. If I wanted to do the rest of level 2 I would have to go to Dover College and study there. But I did not fancy travelling all the way to there and I did not fancy all the things that it involved studying, such as French.

While I was at college we had to move home's, from Pensand House, Hythe to Elm road, St Mary's Bay. On our way to Elm Road we had to sell of our furniture because we were going from an unfurnished place to a furnished place, it was a shame because we had some beautiful pieces of furniture; but they had to go.

David picked me up from college that afternoon after he had delivered all the furniture and taken most of our bits and pieces off at Elm Road. We were glad to leave Pensand House with all the faults it had, it was good to get in to a place that has no faults in it at all, welcome to Elm Road.

This year we had our red mini metro stolen from the car park opposite the police station in Ashford, Kent. We were in the bingo hall playing bingo, we didn't win. Anyway we were in there playing bingo, after we had finished we went out to the car park, to the disabled parking space and it was empty. Our car, it was gone. Where could it be? We went to the police station and told them exactly what happened. When David told them where we lived, St Mary's Bay, the policeman on duty that night said 'Where's that?' I mean it is supposed to be on part of their mapping area and he asks where it is. I don't know what is the world coming to?

We ended up phoning David's step-father Ron up to come and get us, because David did ask if a police car could take me home, it did not matter about himself he could walk home but I could not. The policeman said no but we could phone someone. That was when we phoned Ron. He took us home, I was a bit annoyed because I had a white stick in the front of the car and this meant I had to send off for a new one.

We had no news about the car, I expect it is probably out of the country by now. In a way we were glad that the car was stolen because of the mileage we would have had to pay on it because it was a Motability car. It would have had been up in the £700 and we could not afford that. We had to contact Motability about the car being stolen and getting a new one, we would have to wait six months for a new one to come through. Six months, I can't wait that long. David had an idea to phone up on the radio and see whether they could help, and sure enough they did. This couple were listening to David's plea on the radio and had this mini sitting there doing nothing. So they offered it to David free of charge, and he said yes. So we were getting a mini, until they want it back, which could be about four to five months, which will suit us, fine.

David's mum, Joan had recently got a new dog, a small dog. I fell in love with her as soon as I saw her and I think she liked me too. When I first saw Mitsy (that is her name) I picked her up and she fitted in to the palm of my hand, now that is small.

Joan let Mitsy come away to our house for a holiday. We loved to have her. By the time she came to us she was a lot bigger than she was before. She loved her time in the mini because she climbed up on to the back up against the window and went to sleep.

One time David had a restless night, he took an over dose of tablets because his neck was giving him a lot of pain. Anyway,

David and Mitsy went in the mini at 1am in the morning drove all the way to Tesco's in Folkestone, Kent to do get some cigarettes (which he didn't smoke), but Mitsy was there. So there was David and Mitsy were out shopping, and there was me at home worried because of David taking all these tablets. About 4am David came in with Mitsy behind him. Mitsy did alright because she got some hearts and I got some trouser and socks. In future I am going to keep David keys hidden, somewhere where he can't find them. Hopefully he will never do anything like this again in the future.

1995

The next car we got was a white Corsa M582 OKM. We decided to get this car because this car was more spacious than the car we had before. And that it is what I wanted in a car; space and height. A car must have height because since the car accident, I must have a car that has some height above the opposite cars headlights because I cannot have their lights blearing at me so I cannot see. I really hate that, don't you?

There was one time my Nan Hoy was having problem with my Uncle Ted, I don't know exactly what the problem was; all I know was my Nan was upset. We went all the way up to Bagshot to take my Nan shopping, we didn't mind but my mum lives about 25 minutes down the road from her. Now why couldn't she have taken her?

So my Nan wanted a holiday, time to get away from my Uncle Ted, so we suggested that she came down to stay with us for a while; and she agreed. So she and her friend Karen (a young woman in her 20ist) came down; Karen came down for one week while my Nan came down for two.

They had a wonderful time down here. Karen pushed my Nan about in her wheelchair, whilst I had an appointment up at the William Harvey Hospital, a check-up and David was doing his voluntary driving like usual.

It was a frosty morning, David and I were playing in the kitchen and I attempted to run with David following behind. When suddenly

I tripped and fell banging my head on the way down on the unit in front of me and knocked myself out cold. Of course that made David call for an ambulance and within five minutes an ambulance was there. David explained what had happened and explained my medical history, about my stroke (me having a CVA when I was 16).

The ambulance men took me in the ambulance to the William Harvey Hospital. Meanwhile David was following behind in the car. When we got to the hospital I was just about coming around. They kept me in for 24 hours just to make sure I was alright. I was alright after that; I must stop that game of cat and mouse with David because the mouse keeps on getting injured (trust me).

Another time I had a really bad migraine, I suffer from these at least one a week. Anyway, this time David was out at bingo so he wasn't due back until after 9.30pm, and this migraine was getting worse and worse. When David came in he found me in banging my head against the furniture, crying, holding my head saying to myself 'go away'. So he phoned the doctor up on the emergency line at Lydd, Kent and the doctor said 'bring her over to us over at the ambulance station'. So David made sure that I was ready to go outside; then he took me outside in the car to the ambulance station. Once we got there, he struggled to get me out of the car and in to the ambulance station. Inside there we saw the doctor for a few minutes and he gave me a letter to give in at the A&E at the hospital when we got there. So we had to make our own way there, they were too busy watching football.

1996

It was in this year when my dad had to go up to Scotland to get my Nan Norgate's body because she died up there whilst on holiday with my Great Aunt Emmie. They had gone up there for their Christmas holiday but my Nan Norgate had never finished it.

I think my Nan Norgate must have known that this was her last year because she had brought everyone Christmas presents, which she hadn't done for the past five years since she had fallen out with my mum.

It was a sunny day for her funeral, which had been unusual for this time of year (January). My Uncle Harry, Aunt June and cousin came up from Henfield, whereas we came up from St Mary's Bay to Addlestone, Surrey which was where she was living and it was where her body was going from to be cremated.

We went away for Christmas this year; we went all the way to France. A French friend invited us to come for Boxing Day. We left of Christmas Day at around 5pm, the last boat out. We travelled all night, as far as we could possible go, then I fell asleep. David drove until he couldn't see anything. There was nothing but empty fields everywhere. Then he went to sleep himself. When we both woke up the whole ground was white with snow, we couldn't believe our eyes.

With the ground all with it was almost impossible to see which way we had been before, but we somehow managed. We were getting short of petrol. Somehow we managed to find a petrol station. David got some petrol, and he asked someone if they knew the way to where we were going to. That person was so kind, they not only showed us the way, they took us to the doorstep off our friends, and that was about 5 miles away, wasn't that kind of that person to do that for us.

We arrived at our friends just as they were finishing dinner. They introduced themselves; there was Mireille (our French friend), the mother, the father, the sister and the grandmother (the mother of the father of Mireille). They did offer us something to eat but we both said no thank you, but we would like to rest for a little while as we have been travelling all night, so they showed us the bedroom we were going to sleep in during our stay there.

During our stay there we were shown some interesting things. We were shown some caves where mushrooms were grown. The caves went on for miles, and so did the mushrooms, they grow in all different colours, shapes and sizes. Personally I don't like them myself, but David does and so does the French family, so we brought some for dinner that day or the following day.

The family produce wine products; they produce red, white and champagne wine. All the wines taste very nice. The mother was telling us that once the grapes are all picked all the workers get together and have a festival (like what we call a harvest festival).

While we stayed with Mireille we also visited our other friend. We were invited around to her place for dinner, Mireille came too because none of our other friends' family could speak English so Mireille was our translator. When we all sat down to dinner, we started off with a soup. When we had finished the soup I said to David how nice it was and that it tasted like sardines. David asked what kind of soup it was, and he found out it was lobster soup. Thank god the family couldn't understand English.

When we left their place in France we took two cases of each of their wines, and it didn't cost much money either. Although it was still snowing the roads were still clear because the French are more equipped when it comes to clearing roads. It was like on the main roads from Paris to Calais the road sweepers were three a breast. Now here in England you would be lucky if you would see one road sweeper let along three. And the roads are in utter chaos with one bit of snow, but I hate to imagine what they are like in a blizzard.

It was December when we heard from the council, they have given us a fortnight to move into an unfurnished bungalow out of a furnished bungalow. This unfurnished bungalow was really nice; it was a two bed room place. It had a large sitting room, a small kitchen of that, back off the sitting room was a hall way, off the hall way was a bath room, the spare room and the main bed room. The spare room is big enough to put two single beds side by side and a single bedside cabinet in between them. The bungalow was in New Bridge Way, St Mary's Bay; the only problem was getting furniture.

1997

Before we went away we got some furniture together, some of it was army made furniture made to last, all made with proper joints. The only thing that we brought brand new was the beds, the carpets, the cooker and the washing machine. The rest we got from this house full of army issue furniture; that would have been dumped anyway.

We had the carpets laid before we went away, that was after we had painted the front room because it was a bright orange; it was so disgusting it would have made you feel sick if you stayed in the room to long. The carpet that was laid in the front room was red in colour, the one that was laid in our bedroom was a grey in colour and the spare room, well the carpet that was left behind was alright, so we left that as it was.

The kitchen, now that was a different story. The sink was alright, the cooker was fine and the washing machine was fitted alright it was just the unit on top off the machine that just needed replacing. Now the rest of the kitchen needed redoing and re-decorating. Let me tell you about one of the cupboard's that had the electric and the gas meters in it. You had the gas meter sitting on top off the electric meter and guess what we had a gas leak. And the gas people told us to turn the gas and electric meters off. We told them where they can go. So when they came to fix the leak we asked them to put the both meters outside.

After we got everything settled in our new bungalow we decided we needed a holiday, we decided that we would go to stay with Mireille in France. We thought we have been there once so we know the way so we won't get lost. So what do we do but get lost going round the auto-route (like our M25) round Paris, so we pull over and two policemen on motorbikes pull over. David shows them where we want to go on the map; and the two officers kindly said follow them and they will show us where to go off at the correct junction. Now who said that the French were not nice people, we have been over here twice and both times they have helped us out by going out of their way; now that's what I call kindness.

We spent two holidays over in France this year, because Mireille's family said to us to go over there whenever we wish because their home is always open; that was nice off them. We liked our trips over to see them all, in all our trips over to see them we always took them presents. For instance we took the father a box of cigars, because we know he likes to have a good smoke after lunch and dinner.

This winter I fell ill with my epilepsy, this time it affected my right ankle and right arm/wrist. My ankle took the worst of it, it went right under; but luckily the centre at the William Harvey Hospital, Ashford, Kent had a splint for that sort of thing. The splint for the ankle went up both sides of the leg, it may look funny but it works. Now the arm/wrist, they had splints for wrists but none suitable for what was needed for me, so they had to make one. The physiotherapist that did the splint for my arm/wrist was ever so nice, he was ever so gentle. I had to see him three times because it took time to fit the splint into shape, but he finally fitted it.

1998

The next car we got was a green Astra R61 YKN. We decided to get this car because there was more space in the back of the car than the Corsa and there was more leg room in the front of the car.

It must have been early January when David had gone round the village hall with his mum, Joan. I was waiting in door's for David to come home about 4'ish but instead he came in at about 3.30'ish, I was a bit puzzled. Then David said that his mum has been rushed to hospital because she had heartache in our car next to him. I wondered why he looked a bit pale in the face, now I know why.

We then went over to Ron's (David's step-father) and his mum's house, also where David's Nan was. David told Ron what exactly happened, and Ron said that he would go up to the hospital once he had sorted David's Nan out. We left Ron's and went straight up to the hospital, were we met David's sister Chris.

Joan was in intensive care for about five days; then she was taken on to the wards. She was on the ward for a couple of weeks before she was taken to St Thomas' Hospital in London for a triple bye pass. That went alright, all but one of the metal stents took; but that did not matter.

It brought the whole family closer together, that included David's brothers' Ronnie and George. It also brought David sister from Manchester, Sue down, also came Denis, David's broth-in-law. Chris came down from Harlow in Essex and stayed close by just in case anything happened to her mum.

When Joan was up in St Thomas' we visited her every day, while Chris stayed in the staff quarters because there are some rooms up there for parents or partners to sleep. Joan was getting better all the time she was up the in London. She had improved so much that they said that she could go back to the William Harvey in Ashford, Kent.

Joan left St Thomas' in good time. She arrived at the William Harvey Hospital at about 3pm'ish. Joan was a diabetic so she needed her insulin an hour before she had anything to eat, but the nurses said they did not have anything on paper so they could not give anything to her. We, the family, all say that it should have been written down on paper from hospital to hospital what medication each patient is on, but for some reason it isn't, or it wasn't this time.

It was at one o'clock in the morning when Joan was given her insulin. Chris, David and I we totally discussed at this, but there is nothing that we could do about it. Over the following day Joan was feeling colder, she had six blankets on her and she was still feeling the cold. In the evening she went to the toilet, she was told she must have a nurse with her when she goes to the toilet; she had no body. While in the toilet, she was sick; she cleared it up herself. She must have had a fall while she was in the toilet because she had a large bruise on her leg.

When she got back in to bed she told the nurse that she had been sick; so the nurse gave her a bowl and told her to get on with it. If

I had been there I would have given the nurse a piece of my mind. As it was later that night Joan was rushed back down to intensive care, where as if it didn't help in the bed next to her was her sister, Kath. She was in there suffering with the same thing as Joan was. She was waiting to go up to London to have the same thing as Joan had done.

When Joan was ready to come out of intensive care Chris made sure that she did not go back on to that ward that she was on before, instead she went on to Kings ward because they seemed a nice ward. Joan was on a side ward because she had so many visitors, cards and gifts.

I used to sit with Joan after I had been to my physiotherapy session downstairs in the centre below once a week. Joan used to tell me when her son George came up, that she used to really hate it because she could never tell which mood he used to be in. It was like one time when Joan was in London, George went on a two mile round trip just to get a can of larger/fosters. I mean if you cannot go to see someone without having a can of drink then there is something wrong with you.

It was a sad day when Joan died. David and I went in to see her; she just looked as though she was asleep. I couldn't help myself but cry it was as though I was losing a friend, let alone a mother-in-law. Chris felt so guilty because that morning she had her first lay in for a long time, and her mum happened to die on that morning.

The funeral was a sad occasion, David, George and Ronnie helped to carry the coffin down in to the church and out again. They all had tears in their eyes. I know I cried a lot when she was put in to the Hurst to take her to the crematorium. At the crematorium David and his brothers were going to carry the coffin but the ushers said it would be too much for them, so they just walked behind instead.

This year after we had laid Joan, we made friends with two elderly sisters, May and Agnes. They wanted to go on holiday, so we said we would take them. We ended up going to Devon. The rooms that we were supposed to have only had a bath in it, we asked for a shower because three of us can get down into the bath but cannot get out of it again. So instead of having two rooms they gave us a caravan which had a shower in it, which suited us better.

David had problems while driving down to Devon, he had shingles. It was his first time and only time, we hope. He had it around his right hip, around were his seatbelt goes. So he had to use my sanitary towels for protection against his seatbelt rubbing his side.

The first morning David went to the chemist to see whether he could get some padding for his waist for his shingles. They didn't so he carried on using my towels instead. It was lucky I brought extra towels with me because David seems to be using them more than me.

We went to bingo each night on the camp site, we didn't win a sausage but we enjoyed ourselves. The sisters won once or twice. The two sisters we went with moaned about everything and moaning about each other, but that is enough about the two sisters.

It was also in this year when we took over the bingo from the old gentleman that ran it before us because he was retiring. We brought a new bingo machine, one that showed the numbers that were being called clearly so that everyone could see them.

We started a Christmas raffle with over twenty five prizes, ranging from packet of sweets up to hampers of goodies. We didn't sell as many tickets as we thought we would but you learn from your mistakes.

This December David met Ian who was the instructor for the martial arts group Taekwon-do. David only joined me up to do this Taekwon-do. Yes I do this Taekwon-do. So we went along on a Wednesday evening and I joined in. I spent most of the time on the floor and everyone was helping me up, but I enjoyed myself. I was the only disabled person there and while I was learning of Ian, Ian was learning of me because Ian had never taught a disabled person before.

1999

The Taekwon-do was going fine. In January I was due to take my first grade in. It was held on one of his Sunday sessions when I couldn't make the morning group because we had our bingo instead. In the afternoon we had a quick dash in to Ashford, Kent to the Taekwon-do for the grade in. I made it just in time. Whereas all the others had time to practice, I did not, but I had to go straight in to the grade in.

I failed the patterns but I managed to do all the rest of the things like punches, kicks, defences etc. After the other grade in's had finished we went upstairs and sat down, where Ian gave his verdict. He passed everyone; that includes me. I was over the moon. The first person I phoned was my mum. All she could say was not congratulations but they took your disabilities in to consideration. I went from feeling over the moon down to feeling so low. How could anyone say something like that, especially a mother to a child?

One incident that happened in Taekwon-do, it was no bodies fault, but when I was sparring with one of the instructor's (a black belt) we both kicked at the same time, our feet entangled and I fell back, banging my head on the floor on the way down. This caused a little fit for about 15 minutes, and when I came round I sat up and wanted to start again, but they wouldn't let me. The instructor said about bringing a helmet in for me to wear to protect my head. So from that day onwards I was to wear a helmet to protect my head.

Later on in the year I passed another grade in, so then I was yellow belt green tab, this time I knew better than to tell my mum that I had passed another grade in. The only thing that bothers me is learning all the different names in their language and how to count one to twenty or higher.

With the bingo, we are still doing well. We do one money game and the rest grocery games. Some people asked if we could do it so it was all money, David said that he would look in to it. So David went to see the committee (who did a full money session once a month) and the gambling committee. The gambling committee sent a leaflet back and David read it. You wouldn't believe it even the committee were doing it illegally. So they had to change their bingo or stop it. They soon changed it, not only theirs; they also took over our bingo so that was the end of our bingo. It just was not fair the way they did it. David stayed around for the first Saturday that was supposed to change but there was no bingo because the committee expected David to get all the money in and split it between the two of us, them and us. But we were not having it that way, we decided they can do it all themselves; if they want to! Little did we know they would make a great success of it!

2000

This year I started playing darts. I started playing for the British Legion for the women, the captain is Diane. Diane lives just round the corner; she was like a new mother to me and David and her husband Brian is like a new father to me. In darts I was rubbish to start with and to prove it I got a 'wooden spoon' a trophy. It proves that we got somewhere in darts, even if it is last place.

At darts I started playing for the British Legion in Dymchurch, Kent. There was one person who sat at the bar who I really hated, that was Dick, that person who assaulted me way back in 1988/90. He lived here in Dymchurch and drank in the British Legion. I hated playing at the British Legion because he was always there, I could feel his eyes staring at me, even though I was not looking at him. David had told my darts team all about what he had done, so they knew when to keep out of his way.

Doing this Taekwon-do has given me enough courage to face this Dick. It has shown me how to defend myself which is what I needed when someone attacks me. I can still feel his eyes staring at me and there is his laugh, it is so loud you couldn't mistake it from anyone's. I really hate him, after what he has done to me. I could just imagine what I could do to him, now I do Taekwon-do it has given me enough courage to confront him if I had the opportunity to, but that will never happen, thank god.

My Nan Hoy and Uncle Ted came down to visit me for the weekend, which I thought was nice of them. While they were down David and my Uncle popped into Asda, while my Nan and I sat in the car. I decided to go to the toilet, so I left my Nan in the car and walked into the store. As I came out I went to go around a customer that was at the trolleys. The trolleys were stacked out three a breast, so I went to go around the back of the customer not looking at the right of us I never noticed a large pillar, of course not; I am partially sighted in my right eye so of course I didn't see it. Anyway I walked straight into this pillar. Of course it knocked me out stone cold and cut my right eye brow, and it gave me a massive black eye.

My Nan Hoy came rushing over, like any grandmother would. She was worried sick, but later in the hospital I assured her that I was alright, even though I had a great big black eye. I told my Nan not to tell my mum, I would tell her in my own time. I stayed in hospital overnight but was allowed home next day.

A couple of days later I went to Taekwon-do, not to take part just to watch. As I walked in everyone looked at me as if I had been in a fight or something. I had to assure them that I hadn't been in a fight, whereas I had just walked into a post at Asda. I was off from Taekwon-do for three weeks with this eye, but don't worry when I got back I was as strong as ever.

2001

The next car we got was a green Zafra, which was an X registration plate number. This car was comfortable to sit in and plenty of space to put things in the boot.

It must be this year Diane's daughter Natalie took over from our old cleaner to do our cleaning. She did a better job of doing our cleaning then our old cleaner in less time, and she did our ironing too. Mind you she took our ironing away with her to do it at her home; I suppose she prefers to do it in her own surroundings which is understandable.

This year we went on holiday with Diane and Brian; we went to the Isle of Weight. When we left, we went in Brian's car but something started to go wrong with Brian's car, so we had to come back and get in our car. So we ended up leaving Portsmouth in our car on a ferry heading for the Isle of Weight. It was the first time David and I had ever been to the Isle of Weight. A couple of months before Brian said to me, all seriously, don't forget your passport? A couple of minutes later I realised he was joking, what a Wally he must think I am to think you need a passport to go to the Isle of Weight.

When we got there it was a field with about 50 caravans in it. We found our caravan; it was in line with the main house where the bar was. The bar was not that good because every night we drank something different because they ran out of that drink. For instance, one night we would be drinking larger and the next night that would have run out so we would have to drink something else. We got feed up so we got our own drinks in and drank them back at the caravan.

For entertainment, we visited the Needles, they were nice to see. We went down and saw them through the window in the side of the cliff face. One thing we loved to do is to play crazy golf. We stopped at many places to play this game. I can remember one game that we stopped at and it was this game of shot'n'put. It was a game of one to nine so you had to play it twice to play one to eighteen. The first round went fine; I didn't want to play again so I sat with the bags and watched. When it happened, David hit his ball and it began to roll and roll and roll towards the river. There was a 50 pence fine for each ball that goes in to the river. Now as the ball rolled David ran, his arms waving in the air and his legs from side to side. If only I had a camera. As he was running all three of us were laughing so much, it was hurting our sides. Luckily David did catch his ball, but it was so funny.

On night when we did go to the bar, David was drinking Pernod, blackcurrant and lemonade. He finished the bottle off; mind you there was about half a bottle in there anyway. When we got back to the caravan we started to play our game of cards; when Brian started talking about Harold and that started David talking about Arnold. Brian thought David was joking but David was totally drunk; meanwhile Diane and I were laughing so much that we had pains in our sides.

The next morning David woke up, he couldn't quite remember exactly what had happened last night. Diane, Brian and I all said about Arnold and Harold, and he sort of remembered what had happened.

We only spent a week on the Isle of Weight. A couple of days near the end of our holiday I caught a really bad cold, it was so bad David had to pop in to a chemist the on the island and buy some medication and tissues for me. So apart from me catching a bad cold we all enjoyed the holiday a lot, even the trip back on the ferry to Portsmouth.

2002

This year David surprised me by taking me up to London to have my photograph taken be a professional and to have my make-up done by an artist. We drove the car up to St Thomas Hospital in London; then got the taxi to the place where they were taking the photos because David had no idea where the place was and there was nowhere to park around there.

I must admit I did look good. I took my own clothes to wear though, apart from the one that made me look sexy, they provided the scarf for that one; I just wore it. It did make me look good though, don't you think?

After the photos were taken we were taken into a room and shown the photos on slides. We had to choose seven slides. They cost a lot of money, but as David said I am worth it seeing as it was a once in a life time opportunity and we should take it.

These pictures are four of the seven that were taken at the studio where I was made up to be a star. The first one is of David and I as an extra because the lady who was taking the photos had some spare photos left on the film so she said to David to come in and she will take some of both of us.

After we had been there we headed back home. On the way home we decided to pop in to see Ian to see how I got on in the grade-in that I took a few days before. It was for my green belt (my third grade-in for Taekwondo-do). Ian said that I had failed; I knew that before he even said a word. He said I could have done my kicks a lot more firm; as for my punches they could have been a lot stronger, so you could have said I was totally crap. So I have got to be a lot more firm; and stronger in all my body movements. So next week I have got to be a lot stronger than before; and do you know what I was.

In a few months, I retook my Taekwon-do third belt again and guess what, I passed it. I was so over the moon to have passed because I put so much it to it that a Wally could have passed it. That must make me a Wally. So that means I am a green belt, the next belt I am going for is my green belt blue tab, that is a hard belt but who knows I might get it.

This year we went on holiday with Diane and Brian to Great Yarmouth. David and I have been there before and enjoyed it so much that we wanted to bring Diane and Brian there too. We hired a chalet while we were there, which was one week.

While we were in Great Yarmouth we went on two of the trips. First of all we visited a place like 'Yesterday World'; it had a cinema with the old organ that played the music with the film shown. I thought it was fascinating because I had never seen anything like this before.

The second place we visited was a 'Water Garden'; this was next to a river but was a lake that had pathways up and down, in and out of it, so that you could walk all around it. At the end of it you came to the river, where sat a boat which you could pay to go on to go around the river, which gave a tour on the river life. It was quite interesting.

We were sitting in the chalet when this clip came on about an airplane crashing in to a sky scraper and then another one did the same. Brian and I both stopped what we were doing waiting to see what time this was on, then a few seconds later realising that this was not a film but actually happening. Calling to Diane and David A.B. to come to watch this; they soon came and they couldn't believe their eyes. Well neither could we.

We only stayed in Great Yarmouth for one week, and during that week we used to pop over to the main club building for the bingo in the evenings. Then we used to go back to the chalet to play 'Uno' (the card game), Brian used to jokingly moan because he used to end up with all the pickups, it is just the way it worked out. That is what we always say.

It was after our holiday, David and I had one of our silly arguments. It was one that lasted over night because David slept in the spare room and me in our bed. David got up first and he came to wake me up, I couldn't open my eyes or move my left arm or left leg. I was getting worried, after a few minutes I began to see a little but that was it. I had had a minor stroke; no way near as bad as the first one I had had in 1988.

David had called for an ambulance, which arrived within ten minutes. They took me to the William Harvey Hospital, Ashford. In there they were alright, they didn't do anything special like physiotherapy or rehabilitation, instead they just kept an eye on me over the two weeks I was on the ward. After the fortnight had gone past I was almost back to normal, well as normal as I was before I went in.

2003

The next car we got was a Citroen Berlingo. We liked this car because it was comfortable and it was slightly higher off the ground than the other cars we had before. There was plenty of room inside; it has a shelf above the front window screen and it also had boxes in its flooring in its back flooring. Which meant you could hide things in the floor without anyone knowing it was there.

We went on holiday for the third time with Diane and Brian to a place near Hailing Island, Hampshire. We found our chalet alright, but we were not satisfied with all the workmen and dust going on all around us. We had to keep the windows closed all the time to keep the dust out, and one day we could not use the toilet or any taps because they were turning the water off.

Just down the road from the chalet was a butterfly site that also had a crazy golf on site. We looked around the butterflies, they were beautiful. After we had a drink, then it was time for the golf. It was a bit crazy but it was a laugh.

Another trip we went on was in Portsmouth around the harbour. We would have gone around the docks and around the Mary Rose (the famous boat), but it would have cost over £76 for the four of us. That was for one disabled, one old age pensioner, and two adults. It is so pricey, so we went to see how much the small boat were charging and guess what, they cost a fraction of what it cost around the docks, so we chose those instead.

The small boat showed us more boats than we would have seen if we had gone around the docks. The boats we saw were the big war ships; it was good to see them and to see how big they really are. When we were half way round we stopped at the 'Submarine Museum', where we got off and looked around there. It was an interesting museum. Part of it was to go inside a real submarine; even I had to dunk my head to go through parts of the submarine, but we all really enjoyed ourselves a great deal and I learnt a lot about submarines that I did not know before.

This was the second time David had shingles. He had it on his left leg; it was horrible to look at. He had it before so he knew what to do. Luckily I have never caught it, and I would never like to catch it. Apparently it's like a rash with a burning sensation and it is very painful. According to the doctor you cannot get shingles more than once, I don't think much of this doctor because this is the second time David has caught it.

2004

It was in January when Diane and Brian asked us if we would be prepared to look after Nick in the summer while they go on holiday abroad; we said yes we would love to. As Nick was a foster child we would have to fill in some forms for police check and so forth. We did this in January to give them at least five months to check our records out.

Diane and Brian thought that our papers had been all checked, so had we, seeing as we hadn't heard anything from social services. The week before they were due to go Diane phoned the social services up to make sure it was alright. Social services said that our records have not gone though, so Nick could not go to us, instead he was to go to this children's home. Diane and Brian were furious with social services but what could they do?

They day before they were due to go, they phoned up this children's home to make sure Nick was going there. To their surprise the children's home said 'No Nick cannot go there because the home is full up of refuge children'; so Nick will have to go somewhere else. The only other place for him to go is with us, so that is where he went.

Nick must have been with us for about five days, when Nick's social worker turned up out of the blue. She said that she was not happy with Nick being with us and that she was looking for another place for him to go to. Nick said that if she moved him he would run away from this new home. So she had no option but to leave him where he was. She said that she would pick him up on Friday, just to take him out for a chat; she will be there at 4.30pm.

On the Friday, we waited until 4.30pm and there was no sign of her. She eventually turned up at 5.20pm and David had a go at her, all she said was 'Well I am here aren't i?' I mean that is no way to speak to anyone, especially in front of a foster child. When they came back she dropped Nick off and that was the last we saw of her. We told Diane and Brian about all this when they got back, and they were not very impressed.

It was a warm sunny June and on David's birthday (6th June), his brother George invited us over for a bar-be-q; we said yes we would come.

We arrived over there; it was running mad with children, mainly George's grandchildren and a few of his own children that have already grown up. The only soba one there apart from the children was Mildred; that was because she did not drink.

George was like his usual self, drunk and full of dope. I feel sorry for the little kids because they are shown one side of the fence and not the other, so they don't know what is right or wrong. Anyway at least there is one person in the house hold that has common sense to keep of the booze and that is Mildred.

We did not stay there for too long as we know when to leave and that is when George has had a little too much. So we make up some excuse to get away and make our exit short and sweet.

2005

David had gone round by the old school house in New Romney, Kent, when he noticed that there was a computer class going on inside. So he went inside there and inquired about it, not for himself but for me. He did all this behind my back. So without my knowing I was now a member of this computer class.

When I started I found it quite easy because I had done it all before when I had been to South Kent College in Folkestone, Kent; the only thing I found hard to do was the 'databases', but that was not to come until the OCR Level 2 Certificate for IT Users (New CLAIT).

It was silly who would use half of the things you would do for level 1, I mean I know you would use at least two of the things you would do for level 1. The things that are mainly used for level 1 are Using a computer and Word processing, the thing that are not mainly used are Spread sheets, Graphs & charts and Presentation graphic. Those three things don't appear as an everyday thing.

Now it is the same with level 2, there is only one thing there that really comes to an everyday use; and that is Create, manage and integrate files. The other three don't come into use. They are: Spread sheets, Databases, Graphs and charts. I completed these two exams in the first six months. Meanwhile, there were some workers there and it took them six months to do just the word processing part, and that was the easiest part of it.

My Nan Hoy had been ill for some time; she had been in hospital for quite a while. I was around Ian's when we heard to news that she had died. Trust my Nan to choose a day of days like today to die on because it was the same day as the Pope. The Pope died this morning whilst my Nan died this afternoon.

The funeral was interesting, a bit sad but over all a bit sad. Two of my cousins were there and they told me that my Uncle Ted had sexually assaulted them and they asked me if he had ever done anything to me, I couldn't lie; he had touch me but that was all. They wanted me to go to social services with this information against Uncle Ted. I didn't really want to but until one of the told me one off the cases he had touched her I felt it my duty, but my case seemed so petty compared to theirs.

I did all I said I was going to do. The next thing I knew my mum was on the phone to me saying I was a liar and that Uncle Ted had never been over on such a day. How was she supposed to remember way back then, when I was six/seven; after all I can only remember a few things; and it is things like that that stick in peoples' minds. And it was because of my mum saying that that squashed the case, so my Uncle Ted was let of the key. In a way I was relieved because I really do like my Uncle Ted. I must write a letter to him to apologise to him for the hurt I have coursed him, but I don't know where to start.

It was in June when David had only just been round Diane's the day before about making her a flower box and what flowers she would like in there.

He had just finished making it and was just taking it over to her house across the road. They were out at that particular moment, so David left it round the back in the garden. David heard them pull up in their car, so he went over to tell Diane about the flower box.

About an hour had past when we heard a siren, we thought nothing of it; that was until Aimi (Diane's youngest) knocked at the door. She came in, her face was full of tears she said her mum's died. We just couldn't believe it, Diane dead. Aimi said that she was asleep when she gave a sudden gasp of air and that was it. Emma gave her mum mouth to mouth until the ambulance got there, but it was no good she was gone.

Diane's funeral was lovely; the amount of flowers was nice to see. She had a horse and carriage. The carriage was glass so you could see the coffin inside; it looked so beautiful, all nice and white smothered with flowers from all of her daughters and her foster son, let alone her husband Brian.

I am still doing my Taekwon-do, and at this time I had passed yet another belt. So this time I had passed my fourth grade in, which means that I am now green belt blue tab. The next grade in, blue belt, seems so hard, well harder than the last four, that I don't seem able to do it. I will give it a go though.

In this year things began to get on top of both of us. Nobody would listen to either of us, it did not matter where either of us went people just turned their back and went in the opposite direction, even the doctors. We had even talked about committing suicide, and we were getting very close to doing it.

This one particular Friday, David and I went to collect my repeat prescription from the chemist and it was not there. So David went round the doctors to see where it was, it had not been written. The receptionist then suggested that we make an appointment to see the doctor that evening, he agreed.

During that day we both we were getting all our medication together for our suicide pack. We put our medication into the Camper and drove off; we got as far as Tenterden, Kent. When we got there David got his mobile out and phoned the police up and started to talk to a police man. The police man talked to David who was talked out of the suicide which he was slowly coming out of. But me, well

I was getting angrier and angrier as each minute went past. David put the police man on the phone to me and I just gave him a lot of negative chat back, and gave the phone back to David, and then got up and went into the back of the Camper and got hold of all the medication and went to prepare it all for taking. David had agreed over the phone to meet the policeman at our local doctors' surgery, all he had to do was get me to agree to go there with him too.

He finally got me to agree to go with him. When we got to the surgery there was no one else there so we went straight in to see our doctor. We talked to our doctor about my prescription and what was the matter with the both of us, he actually listened to the both of us. After that we went out of the doctors' room where there was two policemen waiting for the two of us. One of the policemen said something to David; I am not sure what they said, but one of them arrested us. I could not believe my ears when they read our rights out to us. They lead us out of the surgery, and towards the police car. David asked if he could take his car, they said no, he could leave it in the surgery car park. So he did. They drove us up to the mental health unit, in Ashford, Kent.

There we were shown to a waiting room, where the policemen told us to wait for someone to come. About 10-15 minutes later this man and woman came both holding sheets of paper. They mainly talked to David who did most of the talking. The man said that he wanted to keep David in and send me home, I said that was not a very good idea, he took me out of David's ear shot and asked me why I said it was not a very good idea. I said because I knew where all the medication was and I knew what to take. The man said 'that in this case I think we had better keep you in as well'. Instead of keeping me at the Mental Health Centre with David they were going to send me to the one in Margate, Kent. That was only for one night, and then they brought me back to the Mental Health Centre in Ashford, Kent.

When I got to the mental health centre at Margate I was taken upstairs to where there was about a dozen other men and women, some were shouting at each other about something or other. I sat down in an armchair, not saying a word to anyone. Nobody spoke to me, so I didn't speak to anybody. When it came to evening meal, everyone else went and got something to eat, while I stayed seated and did not eat anything. It was about mid-night before I was shown where I was to sleep.

I hardly had any sleep that night; I spent most of the night standing up looking up staring out of the window. I did try to sleep a little but I could not sleep on that bed, so I tried to sit on the floor. I found that more comfortable. Mind you, even though I found that more comfortable I sit could not sleep.

Throughout the night the staff kept an eye on me because I threated to kill myself the day before and for all they knew I could still do it if I had the right drugs or equipment with me; but of course I did not but that did not stop them from looking.

All the next day I spent it in the room that was originally an interview room but was changed into my bedroom the night before. The only time I was free from being watched was when I went to the toilet. When it came to breakfast and lunch, I passed on both of these. That meant that I had not eaten anything since yesterday breakfast, I just didn't feel hungry.

Later that afternoon I was sitting on the bed when I suddenly fell to the floor with a fit, it only lasted a few minutes but they did not know that I suffered with epilepsy, but they did after this one. I came round in my own time, but I was a little dazed as I was sitting up on the bed. The gentleman who was watching me asked me if I wanted anything to eat, I said no thank you. He said how about a little rice; it took a little while for me to agree to a little rice. When he brought me the rice, the first lot I couldn't eat because it had sweet and sour sauce on top of it, and I don't like that. So he went and got me some more. I only had about a third of it and then I was full up, I think he was disappointed about the amount I ate or didn't eat.

I was only to stay at this centre for one night as they found a bed for me at mental health centre in Ashford, which was good for me because I will be closer to David. I arrived at the Ashford centre when it was very dark, so dark that it was all lit up.

When I got inside the centre I was still under watch. It did not matter if I went to the toilet or not, a female staff went in there with me, but otherwise they took turns to sit with me.

On the first night I can remember going to bed and a male member of staff sitting in a chair at the door to watch me. The next thing I think happened was I had an epileptic fit, and the male staff did not know what to do, so they called my husband David up.

The next thing I remember was waking up in a hospital bed in a new room in one of their new wards. It came to dinner time and like I had done before I refused to eat anything. I did this for the next three/four days, so the nursing staff' were getting a bit worried because I was refusing to drink as well. So what they did was put a drip into me, the trouble was finding a vein. You see it is almost impossible to find a vein to put or take blood out of me. I stayed in this hospital bed for about five days; then I was taken back up to the centre up stairs.

I was under watch for two/three weeks, it was a bit annoying especially when you want to go to the toilet especially when you want to go for number two's. It was embarrassing when you can't help it but you do a smelly one, that's when you have held one in for a few days but you can't hold it in for much longer.

I was relieved when I was let of watch and could go where ever I wanted without being watched. Which meant I could do some of the activities that some of the other patients/clients. Some of the activities are like pottery, computer work, a morning walk etc. I did all these activities plus some more.

When I had to see the panel of doctors and social workers they all suggested that if I stayed in for a further fortnight and if I had anything to say to talk to this particular social worker, and they pointed to this social worker.

A fortnight went passed and whenever I wanted to talk to this social worker she was either off work or on night shift, so I gave up. Meanwhile I had written all my feelings down on paper, it seemed easier than saying it, plus I could remember more if I could write it down. One person I won't let read it is David, I do not know why but I will not let him read it at the moment, so I have given it to Brain and Emma, as they were the only people who I could call friends at that time.

After Brian and Emma's visit I felt a lot better, in fact I felt as though I didn't belong in a place like this anymore. The trouble was what or who do I tell that I don't belong here anymore.

David's nephew up in Manchester was having a surprise birthday dinner party and we were invited the trouble was I was stuck in here. I saw the panel and they would not let me out for the weekend for some reason or other. Yet I was still determined to go out this weekend. About two hours before I was due to leave a young doctor (one of their specialists) came up to talk me out of going out this weekend; but I was having none of this I was going and that was that. I was going and that was final.

I left there on the Friday and was told to come back on Monday morning to see the panel to see what they have to say about me going out without their permission.

We arrived at David's sister Sue late on the Friday night. When we got there we stayed up for one cup of tea and a quick chat then we went to bed.

On the Saturday evening we drove our car to the Chinese restaurant, then our nephew wouldn't recognize our car so he wouldn't have any idea his mum and dad would be here. He was surprized when he came in, he thought it was just his family not everybody else, like David and me. It was a nice meal. The only thing that spoiled the evening was his two children putting soap over the handles of the toilet doors so that anybody using the toilet could not get a grip of the handle properly; but children will have their fun. Apart from that it was a nice evening.

On the Sunday before we went home Sue cooked us dinner, which was nice. Mind you, all her dinners are nice. She also cut my hair for me, it needed cutting badly. After she had finished we said bye to everyone then got in our car and headed for home.

On the Monday we left to go up to the centre up at the William Harvey Hospital, Ashford, Kent. We waited in the centre for about three hours before we were seen; there was a lady who was let out a week ago before me. She was seen before me and it was all thumbs up for her.

At last it was my turn to see the panel. I walked in with confidence, which showed the panel that I did not belong in a place like this. I told the panel of my plans to get better and that my husband was going to help me and that I was going to help my husband get better by encouraging him. So all the panel could do was let me go, so that is what they did.

Once I came out of the centre I felt a lot better; I felt as though I was like a bird that had just been let free.

I had been given a fortnights worth of tablets by the centre but I had to get my repeat prescription re-done by the local doctor. So I went to see my local doctor as soon as possible. He changed one tablet but apart from that he did not do anything to the list, so he just did the repeat prescription as the doctor at the centre did it.

I had gone back to playing darts but it was not the same without Diane being there. It just felt empty. I am seriously thinking about leaving and joining another darts team, that's if this other team will have me.

We decided to spend this Christmas and New Year away in Dubai. It was great over there. It was very hot during the day and very sticky during the night. While we were over there we meet up with one of David's internet buddies and his family. We met up with him and his family twice out of the two weeks we were over there.

They wouldn't let us pay for anything even though we had plenty of money and they were hard up.

We sun bathed until about 1pm, and then we went to the shopping centre. It was massive. There was one section for jewellery, this had no price marked on it because you went in and you bartered for it. David got me a lovely necklace, and he only paid a fraction of the price it is worth. It also had a section for clothes and another for food that you eat. It also had a section where you brought your shopping from. It certainly was a lovely place to go to, to do your shopping.

<u>2006</u>

In this year my worst dreams came true; you know that dream that you stand at the head of a coffin and you look inside and you look at the person inside of the coffin and you hate to think of the person; yes it is your mum. Your sweet mum, well in my case not so sweet, my mum she was so big you couldn't even carry her out in the coffin when they announced her dead, they had to push her out on a trolley.

The funeral was sad, I must admit I did cry; although I said I wouldn't but I did. It was held in St Paul's Church, Addlestone the same church I was christened and married in. The only difference with the church now is that it has had its insides all taken out and chairs instead of benches put inside.

I was surprised at the people that turned up for my mum's funeral. There was Molly from the newspaper shop; she closed the shop to come to my mum's funeral that I was surprised at. There was my friend Sandy, with one of her five sisters and her mum, Maureen. Plus there were some other people who I didn't know. After the church service, we had to go to Mortlake Crematorium to cremate her because this was the nearest place that had the largest furnace to take a large coffin like my mum.

I was having problems with my periods; I kept on bleeding none stop. First of all I had to go to the doctors then I had an appointment up at the hospital. At the hospital, I had to see a doctor and he said that there are several ways around stopping the bleeding. There was the coil, something else and the hysterectomy. He asked which one I would prefer I said that we had been talking about this and we had decided that the best choice would be the hysterectomy. The doctor said that was fine and that the nearest would be in about 4-6 weeks, I said that will be fine.

About four weeks' time I went to hospital for a pre-op, which is where they fill in all the forms ready for when you go in. My forms were easy to fill in; the only thing they had to make sure is when you go under for the operation they use the right one; because if they use the wrong one I come out fitting with epileptic fits, which is not a good thing because I end up in intensive care for a few days.

Today is the day that I have my hysterectomy; I have to be there about 9pm. A funny time I know, but it was the time on the letter; my operation is about 11pm. Before the operation they said that it would be painful, so there would be morphine there when and where I need it.

I had the operation, it was no way near as painful as I expected it. The only bit of pain I got was when I started to move to go to the toilet after I was disconnected from the tube that connected you to the toilet tube. It took me several times to go to the toilet each hour; so I had to go about 3-4 times an hour. I was alright going for number ones' but I found it a struggle doing number twos'. But by the second day out of four I finally did it, and what a relieve it was.

I was in there for four days, and they let me go. They said to go back in a week's time to have the pins out; I did not realise how big the pins were. But in a week's time I went back to have them taken out. I lost count after twelve.

Right now is the time that I could do with talking to my mum, but I can't can I because she is not there anymore, because the silly cow is dead. Why did she have to die when she did? Just when I needed her; oh well, life must go on.

In this year I got terrible pains in my chest and down my left arm. I went to my local hospital, the William Harvey in Ashford, Kent; but they did nothing. So as we were driving up towards London anyway we decided to pop in to St Thomas'. I was in the waiting room like all the other people, when all of a sudden I had a fit just as they called my name. How's that for timing?

I was in there for about a fortnight, whilst I was in there I had a number of tests done on me. I know one thing that was not related to any of the problems of the pains in my chest and the epilepsy was on my left hand my fingers kept on going white, it was just the tips of them.

The test was done on the last day of me staying in there. They also did a scan of my heart; that was alright. The scan of my left wrist showed that there was the main vein that was going along and then it suddenly went all narrow for a short time, then it went back to normal. Now because of the narrow part of my vein my blood cannot flow properly, which causes the tips of my fingers to go white and numb. I asked the doctor if there was a cure for this and he said that there was an operation that could fix it or otherwise you could just learn to life with it, but to have the operation it costs money because you have to go private. As soon as I got upstairs into the ward and got dressed I was allowed to go home.

We decided to spend Christmas and New Year away this year, so we decided to go to Egypt. It was warm during the day but very cold at night. It was a lovely place to visit, but the people/beggars were always under your nose; you had to always pushing them away, apart from that it was lovely. The cost was reasonable too, some things you wanted to look at when you wanted to go somewhere quite cheap; but when the beggars were pushing there wear up your nose were quite expensive.

We met one of the workers' of the staff that work in the little shops on the hotel. His name was Michael; he had two workers with him as well. He sold rugs, table clothes and many other things. While I was there I brought a shawl, it was really nice. It came in useful because one of the trips we went on the women had to cover their head with a shawl or something and that is where this shawl came in to play.

We spent Christmas and the New Year out there. The hotel that we stayed in put on a show to celebrate both the New Year and Christmas celebration; we thought both shows were very good. Mind you we did not stay to see all of the New Year celebration show because we had to be up early next morning to catch our coach to the airport.

2007

The next car we got was a red Renault Kangoo GL55. We chose this car because it was the same height as the Berlingo. Another reason why we chose this car was because it was ready and waiting on the forecourt for us to take away. It is a red car and I hate red cars but in this case I will make an exception.

Well my darts team, the British Legion have finally finished, so I finally plucked up enough courage to ask the Bailiff Sargent if I could join them; and they said yes.

So on the Tuesday I went down to the pub and they introduced me to the landlord and his wife, who fitted me out with one of their t-shirts, which fitted nice and snug.

I think I surprised my new team, Helen and Jackie because of my drinking habits. You see, every time they saw me drinking at the British Legion I used to drink coke or soft drinks, but when I ordered my drink I ordered sherry. Now that did surprise them, so now I am known as the sherry drinker. It doesn't bother me.

It was like this Halloween we were playing darts away at the Ship pub in Dymchurch, Kent. When I was drinking my usual drink, sherry and the rest of the team were drinking this green drink, whatever it was they were drinking it threw straws. So Helen suggested that I drink my sherry threw a straw, like a Wally I agree to. I only drank one glass of sherry threw a straw though, because it made me go all tipsy.

By the time the evening was up I was well and truly drunk. Mind you I did win a tube of pringles (potato crisps). I got out of Helen's car alright, and Jackie walked me to the front door. Now I managed to get the key out of my bag fine, it was getting my key into the door that I had problems with, luckily I had Jackie there to help with that. That was after dropping the pringles four or five time before Jackie took the key from me and putting it in the door for me. David was lying in bed listening to all that was going on, not bothering to get out of bed to lend a hand to help me get in.

The next morning I opened the pringles, the top half were alright; it was when I got down to the bottom half I wondered what had happened to them. Then it all came back to me, last night and the pringles and the key, I remember. I am never drinking threw a straw again.

The following Tuesday Jackie had told Helen about the key and pringles, and they are never going to let me live that down. But that is alright, I have a thick skin so I can take it. After all I married David and he is always joking about with me. He has taught me to take jokes about myself because if I can't take jokes about myself then I can't take jokes about life. This is true.

We decided to spend this Christmas and New Year away, so we decided to spend it abroad in Tunisia. The cleaning staffs were so nice and friendly, and that makes a difference when it comes to running a hotel. The entertainment crew were excellent for what they were. They were so funny, when they were supposed to be and serious when they were supposed to be. Now that's what I call entertainment.

Now the cleaning staff, the lady that we had to clean our room was ever so nice, she washed the floor every morning, changed the bed every morning. In fact she did everything you would expect a normal cleaner to do but it is the way she did it that made it special.

2008

This year was a sad year because although Chris (David's sister) had been diagnosed with cancer before she had got rid of it before too, but this time she had been diagnosed with it again but this time it was all over her body. So she had so many months to live.

With the treatment that Chris was having it was making Chris lose all her hair, the poor thing, I feel so sorry for her; I would hate to have to go through that. As Chris knew that she was going to die she planned her funeral, she even planned her coffin and what hymns she wanted sung and what music she wanted played. She had it all planned, Phil her ex-husband was going to pay for it because he still felt something for her even though they were divorced.

Chris's final week was a sad week. She was in hospital but she wanted to spend he final week at home, so she was brought home. Her daughters: Nic, Lisa and Aimee, and her granddaughter Jodie, all nursed her as well as looked after their own families. David and I visited every day.

The day came for Chris's funeral. We picked Ron up from Lydd, Kent to go up to Harlow, Essex. We got stuck in a traffic jam on the way up there, but we arrived just in time as they were going to leave. Our niece Nicki had arranged with one off the family friends' to take me as David was going in one of the black cars that Chris had set aside for her brothers and sister and Ron, she had also set two black cars: one for her children and one for her grandchildren.

When it came to carrying the coffin into St Stephens' Church David, George, Phil and Denis did the honour of being four of the six people to do it. The church service was nice; Chris had set it out nicely. After that we followed the coffin out of the church and went on up to the crematorium.

This summer we decided to go to Tunisia after all, there is nothing holding us back now. We have no ties to keep us down so we might just as well just go for it. The temperature out there is in its 90's, so we better make sure that we take plenty of sun cream with us.

2009

The next car we got was a grey/blue Mazda 5 GF58 YBW. The day after we picked the car up we headed for Gatwick, because we were due to fly off to Tunisia for a three week holiday in the sun. Sod the cold winter weather we prefer the nice warmth of the sunny weather of Tunisia.

This year we spent January and June/July out in Tunisia; we made some friends with some of the staff and some of the other guests. In the January holiday we got off the plane in Tunisia and the sky didn't look to promising. We went through the check-in desk and got our luggage and came out the other side and all of a sudden it was a thunder storm, the rain was coming down so hard, the thunder and lightning was so wild it was unbelievable, even our suitcases got wet. That shows how hard the rain was. By the time that we got to the hotel it was all sunny again but you could see some of the puddles where the rain had been.

When we came back it was in the middle of the night and guess what we had problems with our brand new car, it would not start. Luckily for us there was a warden going around in his van and he fixed our car. It was just where it was new the battery had not charged up enough to start, so the chap started our engine and told us to go and see our garage tomorrow. So with the car all up and starting we finally got on our way home. The time being 1.40am and we had an hour and a half drive ahead of us before we got home.

It was in December when we decided that we should pay some of that money back that we borrowed of David's real dad Tony, so we went up to see him in his flat in Folkestone, Kent. We went with us £1000 in cash to give to Tony. Tony seemed pleased to receive the money. We took Tony out to lunch once a week that is before we went away on holiday. He seemed quite happy in all the different places that we took him, and afterwards we took him to the Bailiffs

Sergeante, St Mary's Bay, Kent. Which is my local pub who I play
darts for. Tony knew one of the staff that worked there from way
back, so he found someone to talk to.

2010

It is January and we are going on holiday to Tunisia for three
weeks. It is lovely weather, like an English summer. We come out
here twice a year because we love this place so much. We get on
with all the staff and we treat them with manners and hopefully they
will treat you the same back.

In January we met two people named Brian and Valarie, they
we not married just good friends. Valarie lives down Devon way,
whereas Brian lives up London town. Brian must be well off or
something because he pays for himself and Valarie to have six weeks
there in Tunisia. Valarie said that six weeks is a bit much for her, she
said she would prefer a three week holiday instead.

David is such a sweet heart because you see I have got a thing
for white gold and he has brought me a new wedding ring made of
white gold. My original wedding ring which I wear on my right little
finger, anyway where was I oh yes, David being such a sweet heart
because he brought me a white gold necklace for my birthday, which
we spent away in Tunisia. I was 38 years old, I can't wait until I am
40, I don't know why but I can't wait, I want to have a party at home
but who knows what will happen.

On my birthday I had a good birthday present, a trip to the dentist
out there in Tunisia. It was a nice friendly dentist, nice and clean. I
had one filling and one tooth taken out. Also will I was on holiday
in Tunisia another filling fell out but he never did anything with that
tooth. But with the filling and tooth he took out he didn't charge too
much, which I was surprised at because I thought dentists charged
a lot.

When we came home Britain was in a stand still because it was
snowing. It had been snowing and it had turned to ice, then it had

snowed again on top of that. It even had snowed in St Mary's Bay, Kent. Which is a rear thing to do, but it had only lasted for a few days.

After we had been home a few days we went to the travel agents to book our next holiday to Tunisia. It seemed silly booking up for our summer holiday so soon after coming back from our winter holiday, but we had the money there to pay for it so why not pay for it. I mean we don't smoke or drink, so why not use the money to pay for a holiday? So that is what we are doing. The dates that we are going to be away are 16th June until 8th July early hours in the morning.

It was time for our summer holiday, and we are going to spend our 19th wedding anniversary out there. I am going to look forward to next year when we spend our 20th out here we will make it seem so special between the both of us, not that we don't anyway.

I made friends' with a friendly member of staff called Ali-G; he is married with two boys, in fact his wife has just had his second child. He said to me he was not getting enough sleep because his baby boy was crying so much during the night. Ali-G wanted to stay friends so he gave me his address and phone number, so I gave him mine. I will write to him as soon as I get home.

While we were there during the summer holidays David and I went into the Jacuzzi department where I had four types of massage performed on me per day for four days, whereas David had four types of massage, but had one each day. The reason why David only had one a day is because his blood pressure was high each day and the doctor on the centre said that he could not do most of the massage things, whereas I could do any of them I wished, so I had the choice of five different massages. I enjoyed them very, very, very much.

Back to earth, or should I say back to normal life. One thing that I enjoy most about coming back to home is your own bed; you can't beat your own bed. The comfort of the sheets and the mattress, it is sheer utter bliss.

One thing that we learnt while we were away on holiday was that our usual travel agents' was not going to be going to go to our hotel Royal Kenz, Tunisia anymore, so that we would have to go there by another travel agents' that have now taken over the hotel. So the next day we went to Ashford, Kent to the nearest travel agents' to see about our next holiday in January 2011.

The way the travel agents' have organised our holiday is great because once we have got on the plane and got to Tunisia and got off in Tunisia, we get a taxi at the airport to the hotel, and at the end of our holiday we get picked up by a taxi and taken to the airport by taxi. It seems great; there is no sign of any coaches, thank god because I get a bit wheezy on the trip by the coach.

We have organised our transport to the airport from home, we are going by taxi. Well it works out less by taxi than it does by parking at the airport, so we are saving some money by booking by taxi.

A couple of weeks after we came back from our holiday, we were walking out towards the car, when all of a sudden I had a black-out and fell down. I cut both my knees, the palm of my left hand, the top of my right hand and very badly bruised my right wrist. I thought I might have broken the right wrist, well I visited the Royal Victoria Hospital, Folkestone, Kent there walk in centre and saw their head nurse. She was the one who said that it was broken (without an x-ray), so she put a plaster on it. It was a funny looking plaster; I have never seen a plaster looking like this before. She never put a stoking on it first but instead she just put the cotton wool on first, then the plaster of Paris on top, but that only covered half of it. Then she let me go saying to me to come back in three weeks to take it off.

Well four days had gone by and I was getting suffer pain in my right wrist, so David decided to take me up to the William Harvey Hospital, Ashford to let them have a look at my wrist. The nurse that took the plaster off my wrist said that she had never seen a plaster like that before. For starters she said that there was no stocking on it, second, the way the nurse had put the cotton wool on was wrong, she had put most of it around the wrist so that it was weighing the plaster down on what was supposed to be protecting it. And third, the plaster, well that was wrong it was not even protecting anything so that was a waste of time having it on there anyway.

So this new nurse sent me for an x-ray; that came back fine. I hadn't broken any bones but I badly bruised my wrist instead, so the nurse just put my arm in a sling and told me to take a couple of paracetamol if the pain gets to server, and with that she let me go. I was lucky it was not my left hand otherwise I would have been in the s**t (excuse my French) because only having the use of one hand you tend to relay on that more than ever. If someone came up to me and offered me the use of my right hand I would probably say to them no because I have gone 22 years without the use of it and have managed fine without it. But no one would ever come up to the likes of someone like me.

It was July when we heard of Tony's fall in Folkestone, Kent. We heard about it when he had another fall in the hospital and bashed his left check and eye on a table. The state of him it looked like Tyson had bashed him let alone a table. He was a bit unsure of his surroundings and of the people in it, especially me. For some reason or other he kept on having a go at me, it was rather upsetting for me but I didn't let it show.

David's dad was let out of respite about the middle of October and David never missed a day, he visited him no matter what the weather was like rain, wind, snow whatever David was there. I go with him most days except Wednesdays because I go to a computer club. Towards the end of his stay in respite he was getting used to me, the only trouble now was I was going to have get used to the fact that he was going to keep on telling me to 'shut up' even though I have not said a word, so I just laughed it off because I know it was only a joke.

On the 23rd October I was rushed to hospital with epilepsy. Well it all started a couple of days before I got pains in the centre of my chest and down my left arm, so David called for an ambulance. They came and did their business, took my blood pressure, etc. They gave me a little spray under the tongue and that eased it a bit. Then they took all my details off David then they got me ready to put me into the ambulance. At the hospital they just took my heart readings, blood pressure etc. After being in there for about 3 hour they said I could go home. They didn't say what was wrong with me just to go home.

So on the 24th October I was rushed into hospital with epilepsy, the first lot for four years, and it is all due to the signs of the pains in the chest a day ago. The same pains that I had four years ago previously. They only kept me in until Monday evening because I am not on any medication for epilepsy so there is nothing they can do for me, so they might as well send me home. The day that I came out of hospital, Monday, I was still having fits but that didn't matter, because I was still coming out of hospital.

The trouble with epilepsy it wears you out so much for a couple of days so that you cannot do anything you would normally do, like darts. So on the Tuesday after I came out of hospital I felt like s**t, I felt as though I couldn't do anything, so David texted Helen and told her what had happened and said I would not be able to go to darts, Helen texted back ok hope she gets better soon. I was alright the week after.

Since I had a hysterectomy back in 2008 there was no chance of me of having any children, but then there was a ray of light that shone down upon my computer. It happened when I opened my computer up on to my 'Able Here' web page for disabled people and their careers. And there he was, Adnan Sana, he described himself as a midget; and he described me as his mom. As I am the right age, he is aged 20 and I am 38, so that would have made me 18 years old when I would have had him. But the thought of having a son made me so happy; it made me so happy that I felt like I was on cloud nine.

David had also been talking to some people on 'Able Here'; there was one person in particular a woman called Donna. Donna was a 47 year old woman who suffers from cerebral palsy. I have spoken to her once on the internet, and she seems such a nice person. One day she sent David a nice poem that she made up herself. I read it and thought why not share it with everyone else; and here it is:

THANK YOU FOR THE GREATEST GIFT EVER

Thank you for giving me the greatest gift that you could ever give me in my life
Your friendship means the world to me
If I loose it, it would cut through my heart like a knife
Meeting you is a dream come true
You make me so very happy when I feel sad
You give up your time just to talk to me
And that is so very kind of you
You make my days feel so good
When they feel so bad

You are such a kind person making friends with you was easy
You cheer me up when I am down
You are a great friend to have around
We became friends through the Internet and the day I met you
Was the day I met a friend so very, very true
Thank you for giving me so much of your time
When I am talking to you
You always make me feel on cloud nine
Our friendship is like no other I have known before
It is a friendship so define
So genuine it is like a fine wine

Thank you for the greatest friendship ever
Please say it will end never
My biggest wished is that one day we can meet
Face to face so that I can tell you what your friendship really means to me
But for now I want you to know
That you have made me the happiness person that I could be
You have made my days so much happier
And I want to thank you for the greatest gift ever

It is good, don't you think? It is amazing that there is so much talent in such a dark corner, I mean I could never have written such a work of art as this.

This Donna also sent us a Christmas card which she made herself with the help of her computer. She wrote the poem inside all by herself, which went like this:

Christmas time is for giving not only gifts but love
To your family and friends who means so much to you
At Christmas time it's a time to share laughter and memories
So this card I'm sending
To let you know
You will be in my heart and mind
This Christmas time and throughout
The coming new year

MERRY CHRISTMAS

I thought that the two poems were really good and Donna should write a book, and guess what she is already going to write one. I don't know when but I know she is going to.

This Christmas we have been invited to David's Aunt Jenny and Uncle Roger's for our dinner, David got an invite from the email/computer the other morning. He said that we would be having for starters pawn cocktail, for main course veal and vegetables' and I expect for pudding we will be having Christmas pudding.

It is Christmas day morning, it might be 1am in the morning but its' still Christmas morning, and we can open our presents. I said to Natalie that I would wait until Christmas until I would open my presents, and I have. We got a clock, candle sticks and a flower stand of Natalie. David got shower gel and aftershave while I got a watch and necklace of his sister Sue and brother-in-law Denis. My Dad sent us both a gift voucher worth £20.

We left about 9.40am to pick David A.B.'s Uncle Dennis up to take him with us to his Aunt Jenny and Uncle Roger's. We arrived there at quarter past ten; I was already with my red and white Santa's hat. After we had all seated down and had a cup of coffee, Jenny went through the menu; we all had pawn cocktail. Then there was veal cooked with cranberries and something else, I didn't like that; the veal I liked it was the cranberries, so Jenny cooked mine in something else, something I liked. Then there was Christmas pudding; most people wanted mince pies and there were two of us that wanted Christmas pudding with custard. That was dinner. The crackers were different, instead of being toys, they were bells and at the end of the meal you could play a tune because each bell had the number 1 to 8 on it and there was a song sheet with the numbers on it, and you played your bell when your number came up. I thought that was quite good.

After dinner we sat down and played with the bells for a while. Then we opened each other's presents. We got £20 worth of music shop gift vouchers; that can only be spent in one type of shop; we didn't mind, we had to go into Folkestone town shopping centre anyway.

At about 7.30pm we sat down for tea, to tell the truth I was still full up from dinner, but I made an effort. For tea we had three types of cheese, salad, bread, pickle onions, plus something else. I only had bread and cheeses, if I had anything else I would have had felt uncomfortable.

We left there about 9.45pm, after we had said our goodbyes' to Jenny, Roger and Tony. We said to Tony that we would see him again on Friday (New Year's Eve). By the time we got home it was quarter past ten, time I was in bed.

It is New Year's Eve; we went round Tony's, just for an hour. Tony is just like his usual self always telling me to 'shut up' in his usual way, I just tell him to 'shut up' back in my joking fashion way; and we just laugh, then David A.B. starts, then we all giggle.

We phoned Ron up early to wish him a happy new year as we would not be over to wish him a happy new year; instead we had an early night. Instead of visiting Ron we asked him over for dinner tomorrow; and he said yes.

2011

So Ron came over for dinner on New Year's Day. We had a three bird roast, it was lovely. It was the first time Ron had ever tried this before. It consists of turkey, chicken and duck; it was lovely and it only cost £9.99 from Alde from Hythe, Folkestone.

On the 9th January we went on holiday to Tunisia. The taxi came for us at 10am, like we requested. The taxi driver was nice and pleasant; which I feel helps when you drive for quite a long distance.

When we got to the airport the taxi driver dropped us off at the entrance and told us that this will be where he will be when he picks us up. We said that's fine with us.

We went up the escalators in to the departure pad; when we got there we got into the Thompson cue and straight through. After that we went through the area where they check your hand luggage and your coats; ours was all clear.

By all this time I was dying to go to the toilet and the only toilets we could see was up by the restaurants', so we had to go up there. After I had been David and I decided to have something to eat, so we popped into this restaurant that did an all-day breakfast; the only problem with this when David went up to order this was it was too late to have an all-day breakfast. So he ordered a brunch instead, which was like an all-day breakfast except it had chips with it.

After we had brunch we went to see where the disabled seated were seated. As we found it I recognized a face, it was an old gentleman from our hotel last year. Alfred was his name, he recognized us too; well who could forget us.

I bet you have never heard of this before but the front row of the plane the six passengers all going to the Royal Kenz Hotel and all disabled, how about that!

We arrived at the hotel at 8.55pm (Tunisian time); the trouble was David could not eat for another hour due to his diabetes. Luckily we have got some fruit up in the room so David could have some of that. But in the mean time we had a drink in the bar to welcome us to the hotel.

We went down to the Spa and to the Gym next morning to see about taking part. The Spa we started on the Wednesday 12th January and I was due to finish on Saturday 15th January. The Gym we could start today (Tuesday 11th January) this afternoon at 2.30pm. This afternoon we started off by doing 20 minutes on the treadmill and 20 minutes on the exercise bike. Out of the two I prefer the exercise bike.

It was Saturday morning about 5.55am; I don't think anybody had any sleep last night, not with the goings on; with the shooting of that man outside the hotel over the past couple of days. We went down for breakfast, taking our cases down with us at the same time. Breakfast was not much because the hotel did not get its supply through because of all the fighting.

We did not get to leave the hotel until 1pm. We only got about 3 miles down the road, when we were stopped by a soldier, who got on board our coach. We thought that he was going to escort us to the airport but instead he got off a little way down the road where his friends were. We turned round and headed back to our hotel; we were told that we could not go any further because of the prisoners had either broken out of the prison or had been let out. Anyway there was shooting across the two sides of the roads, so we could not pass without being shot at.

Back at the hotel we waited there for a couple of hours; then we were sent to another airport. This airport was not due to open until

April 2011. At this airport there was hundreds of people all waiting to get out of Tunisia; there was people of all nations not only British.

We finally got onto a plane at about 11.45pm but there was a problem with the take-off procedure or something like that, so that meant it would be later than planned. So we finally managed to take-off at 12.10am.

The flight was nice; we had a choice of seats because there were 100 spare seats so that we could spread out. Thompson, the company who we were going with, supplied us with a free meal; which was delicious, which makes a change.

When we got on to this plane we were told that we would not be going to Gatwick Airport but instead we would be going to East Midlands Airport, and from there we would be getting on a coach either to Manchester or Gatwick. We got on the Gatwick coach. It was a long journey to Gatwick but three hours later we arrived there. Mind you on the coach on the way home we had to put up with the emergency alarm keep going off because there was something wrong with the back emergency door.

When we had landed we had to collect our luggage and then head for the coaches, we had to make sure that we got on the right one, as there was one for Gatwick or there was one for somewhere else. We wanted the one for Gatwick.

We got in to Gatwick for about 5am. We got our luggage out of the coach and headed for the taxi station which was up in the main part of the airport. David asked for a taxi to Romney Marsh, Kent and how much it would be. The man on the desk said that it would cost £129 for a taxi to Romney Marsh. We said that would be fine; I expected it to be more expensive, so I was surprised. We finally got home at 8am, which was a long day from yesterday and the day is not over yet.

We finally finished all the days' chores (like washing the clothes, etc.) And got in to bed by about 9pm, and David followed shortly.

For my birthday, I was really looking forward to having that French meal in that hotel on holiday, but it flew out of the window like the holiday. David made up for that by taking me out for a meal in Ashford, Kent. He took me to a pub in Ashford high street. We have not been there before; if we have it has been a long time since we have been in there. David had scampi and chips, while I had liver and bacon. David enjoyed his, whilst I was not impressed with mine. Put it like this I wouldn't go back there again.

The other Sunday I had a text message from my Dad, just to say that my brother Kevin had become a father again, he had become a dad to a boy, whippey. It's not as even if I am interested, which I am not. It is the fourth child he has had. I have been a God-mother to his first one. I was one of six God-parents; he had three God-mothers and three God-fathers. I don't know why he had that many God-parents a bit of waste of time if you ask me.

This Friday's David's father's Tony's 79th birthday, he said that he does not want to go out for a meal, like we planned, because he said he could not eat their size meals which I agree with because I can't eat too big a meal too, so we are getting him a bottle of vodka instead. Tony enjoyed himself very much with the vodka.

For my birthday Donna sent me a Tesco's voucher worth £20 and a birthday card, handmade. I brought some tops with the voucher Donna sent me, they were really nice.

The Mazda Company called all the cars in because there was something wrong with the car, there was something wrong with the power steering. I am glad they called the car in because who knows what might have happened if they have left it. It took them three hours to fix, but as they say 'better safe than sorry'.

It's Valentine's Day. We had said to each other that we wouldn't buy each other a card, but what does David do but buy me a Valentine Card. It was lovely, but I feel so mean because I did not even buy him a Valentine card or anything. What a Meany I am. Mind you there is always his birthday, it is a special one this year, he is 50 years old; half a century. Now it is not every year you celebrate that birthday is it?

My dad text me in March to thank me for his birthday card, he also told me that my Uncle Ted had been charged for drunken driving. This is his third time for this offence. He has to go to court on the 17th March 2011, I think he should be sentenced after all the times he has gone out driving drunk, they should lock him up and throw away the key.

I phoned my dad on the 17th March to see if he knew how Uncle Ted got on in court. He phoned a short while later and said that my Uncle Ted got bound over to keep the peace for a year and a £400 fine. My dad said that he corrected my dad when he was saying that it was his third offence, when in fact it was his fourth. My dad and I couldn't believe it and he only got bound over to keep the peace, if I had been the judge I would have sentenced him. Well at least he has got something; he has to find a new job because he has lost his driving licence which also means losing his job.

It is like the next best thing we have to look forward to, is our anniversary, which is on the 22nd of June, and this year, 2011, will be our 20th anniversary. We said to each other that it does not seem like 20 years it seems longer because of all the things we have been through, but who knows what the next 20 years will bring.

At the beginning of my book I started with a poem written by a blind English teacher called John Dennett. He has helped me with my book by being my proof reader, if it was not for him you would not have the wonderful poems in this book. Thank you John.

If I Could

If I could only look beyond the moon and sky 'oh I wish upon that disappearing star'
I would stand and let it take me to wherever all the stars unite which create the beautiful light that laminates our night;
If I could only see as far as the eye could see, I would follow the shimmering cloud of foam as it leaves the dancing waves that frolic across the sea as far as the naked eye can see;
If I could stand and see through the expense of time, I would for a flickering moment take back my mind and the forever losses of mine which were a part of my former time;
If I could only glance at his disappearing powerful birds wings as they carry his proud beak across the highest peck dancing, daring and beckoning me to follow them the naked eye;
I would take his challenge, and give it my best fly;
Alas! My body and eyes remain dim, and only have the strength and vision that comes from all of them;

So, I am only just Joanna that wishes If I Could, but will do only what I can, as you gently guide me softly whispering that I can because, if I could, I always can.

If you have any enquiries please contact me on my email address:
joannabarnes_227@fsmail.net

I hope that this book gives inspiration to other disabled people........
....
....

I have a lot of respect to other disabled people knowing how hard it
is to cope at time. ....
....